HUMAN RIGHTS AND LEGAL DEFENSE IN NORTHERN IRELAND:

The Intimidation of Defense Lawyers

The Murder of Patrick Finucane

February 1993

Lawyers Committee for Human Rights
330 Seventh Avenue
New York, New York 10001
Tel: (212) 629-6170
Fax: (212) 967-0916

Washington Office: 100 Maryland Avenue, NE
Washington, DC 20002
Tel: (202) 547-5692; Fax: (202) 543-5999

Printed in the United States of America

Lawyers Committee for Human Rights

Since 1978 the Lawyers Committee for Human Rights has worked to promote international human rights and refugee law and legal procedures in the United States and abroad. The Chairman of the Lawyers Committee is Marvin E. Frankel; Michael H. Posner is its Executive Director; William G. O'Neill is the Deputy Director; and Arthur C. Helton is the Director of its Refugee Project.

Copies of this report are available from:

Lawyers Committee for Human Rights
330 Seventh Avenue, 10th Floor
New York, New York 10001 USA

ISBN # 0-934143-58-7

TABLE OF CONTENTS

PREFACE

This report examines two matters of serious concern involving the legal profession in Northern Ireland. The first is that defense attorneys in Northern Ireland continue to be subject to official abuse and intimidation. The second is the still unsolved killing of Patrick Finucane, a prominent Belfast solicitor active in defense and civil rights practice.

This study is based on information gathered during a Lawyers Committee fact-finding mission by John J. Gibbons, Chief Judge (retired) of the United States Court of Appeals for the Third Circuit and Richard J. Hughes Professor of Law at Seton Hall University; Michael Posner, Executive Director of the Lawyers Committee; and Martin Flaherty, Associate Professor of Law at Fordham University. Our mission in Northern Ireland lasted from August 28 to September 4, 1992, and also brought some or all of us to Dublin, London, and Newcastle-Upon-Tyne. One member of our delegation also went on a preliminary fact-finding mission to Northern Ireland. Throughout these visits we attempted to solicit a wide spectrum of viewpoints on the issues we examined. We further did extensive advance and follow-up research. This report was written by Professor Flaherty and edited by Professor Gibbons and Mr. Posner.

During our stays we interviewed solicitors, barristers, former detainees, journalists, government officials, police officials, and human rights activists. Among the officials with whom we met were John Ledlie, Nicholas Perry, David Lavery and David McIroy of the Northern Ireland Office; Michael McAtamney, Deputy Chief Constable, and William McGookin, Chief Information Officer, Royal Ulster Constabulary; John Stevens, now Chief Constable of the Northumbria Police; Justice Ian Higgins, Royal Courts of Justice; John Leckey, Coroner for Greater Belfast; James Grew, Chairman, and Brian McClelland, Secretary, Independent Commission on Police Complaints; Charles Hill QC, Chairman, and Dennis Carson, Secretary, Standing Advisory Commission for Human Rights; and Viscount Colville of Culcross QC, who is a special advisor to the government on emergency legislation in Northern Ireland. Most of these interviewees spoke on the record. We have, however, decided to keep the names of certain sources confidential either at their request or out of concern for their safety. We have also decided not to cite certain journalists by name in light of the recent prosecution of Ben Hamilton of Box Productions for refusing to disclose the identity of a source used in a television documentary about Northern Ireland which he and his company made.

Prior to publishing this report we submitted draft copies to officials in the Northern Ireland Office, the United Kingdom government department responsible for Northern Ireland affairs, and in the Royal Ulster Constabulary (RUC), the Northern Ireland police force. We have included their responses as appendices, and made several changes throughout the report to reflect their comments.

Certain general observations concerning the official responses set forth in the appendices are nonetheless appropriate with regard to the comments from the Northern Ireland Office (see Appendix A). First, we evaluated the allegations that were made to us concerning government misconduct, considering whether the allegations were sufficiently numerous, mutually consistent, and independent to be *prima facie* credible. As a second and closely related point, we conclude that the accounts we heard constitute sufficiently credible evidence to merit an independent inquiry into certain reported instances of official misconduct. Only the government has the authority to administer oaths, issue subpoenas, and conduct a full investigation and prosecution. In the end, authorities must be willing to conduct meaningful inquiries in sensitive cases such as the murder of Patrick Finucane and independent inquiries to determine whether persistent allegations of certain types of misconduct are true or false.

With regard to the comments from the RUC (see Appendix B), the Deputy Chief Constable states that, "[i]t is a pity that notwithstanding the assistance made available to the compilers of the report, that the result should be so flawed." In fact, despite repeated efforts on our own part to gather evidence from the RUC and other authorities, we received no assistance from either the RUC or other authorities regarding the Finucane investigation or alleged intimidation of defense lawyers. The RUC refused to discuss either subject.

Given the complexities of Northern Ireland, our mission would not have been possible without substantial help and cooperation from many quarters. Especially helpful was the Northern Ireland Office, which facilitated numerous official meetings. Additionally, on January 23, 1993, Sir Louis Blom-Cooper QC wrote to inform us of his appointment as Independent Commissioner for Holding Centers and his responsibility to serve as an independent check that persons detained in interrogation centers on suspicion of paramilitary activity are treated fairly. His appointment is a positive development. We also received the assistance of British and Irish government officials in Great Britain, the Irish Republic, and New York City. We also met with and received assistance from Douglas Archard, the United States Consul-General in Belfast.

We also record our gratitude to the family and former associates of Patrick Finucane. Finally, we are thankful for the assistance of other human rights organizations already familiar with the matters we investigated. In particular, we wish to acknowledge the work of an earlier delegation of lawyers who investigated the Finucane murder under the auspices of Liberty (the U.K. National Council for Civil Liberties). We also thank Jane Winter both for her time in meeting with us and for her exhaustive work on these issues for British Irish Rights Watch. Most of all, we record our debt to the Committee on the Administration of Justice in Northern Ireland, especially Martin O'Brien, Michael Ritchie, and Liz Martin who rendered invaluable assistance before, during, and after our time there.

John J. Gibbons
Michael Posner
Martin Flaherty

New York
February 1993

ACRONYMS

EPA	Northern Ireland (Emergency Provisions) Act of 1991, a law which applies only to Northern Ireland
ICPC	Independent Commission on Police Complaints, a commission created in 1988 and appointed by the Secretary of State for Northern Ireland to oversee investigations of complaints regarding police conduct
INLA	Irish National Liberation Army, a republican paramilitary group
IRA	Irish Republican Army, a republican paramilitary group
NIO	Northern Ireland Office, the U.K. government department responsible for Northern Ireland, headed by the Secretary of State for Northern Ireland
PACE	Police and Criminal Evidence (Northern Ireland) Order, applicable to "ordinary" criminal offenses.
PIRA	Provisional Irish Republican Army, a republican paramilitary group
PTA	Prevention of Terrorism (Temporary Provisions) Act of 1989, a law which operates throughout the United Kingdom
RIR	Royal Irish Regiment, a division of the British Army recruited in Northern Ireland, the successor to the UDR
RUC	Royal Ulster Constabulary, the Northern Ireland police force
SACHR	Standing Advisory Commission for Human Rights, a government-appointed independent body which advises the Secretary of State for Northern Ireland on human rights concerns
UDA	Ulster Defence Association, a loyalist paramilitary group
UDR	Ulster Defence Regiment, a division of the British Army recruited in Northern Ireland, subsequently replaced by the RIR
UFF	Ulster Freedom Fighters, a loyalist paramilitary group
UVF	Ulster Voluntary Force, a loyalist paramilitary group

HUMAN RIGHTS AND LEGAL DEFENSE IN NORTHERN IRELAND

SUMMARY OF FINDINGS

General

- There are two principal emergency measures applicable in Northern Ireland: the Emergency Provisions (Northern Ireland) Act of 1991 (EPA) and the Prevention of Terrorism (Temporary Provisions) Act of 1989 (PTA). These provisions are cornerstones of a system designed to obtain convictions in cases involving those suspected of paramilitary activity, based on confessions obtained through prolonged detention and intense interrogation.

- The rights of those suspected of involvement in paramilitary activity are further undermined by attacks against their lawyers. Only a small number of solicitors in Northern Ireland specializes in defense work. Because of the attacks they face, still fewer choose to take politically sensitive cases.

A. Allegations of Intimidation

- Most allegations of threats against lawyers focus on police detention centers. According to former detainees and their solicitors, detectives conducting interviews in such centers bully or threaten detainees, and often make disparaging or threatening remarks about the detainee's solicitor. Among the forms of alleged harassment or intimidation about which we received information are these:

Death Threats

- The most serious allegations of harassment involve death threats. Almost every solicitor interviewed by the Lawyers Committee mission related stories of death threats. Solicitors who once considered such threats as no more than improper interrogation techniques take them more seriously following the murder of Patrick Finucane, a prominent Belfast defense solicitor.

Interference with the Attorney/Client Relationship

- A number of sources told us that police authorities constantly try to drive a wedge between clients and solicitors. Often they allegedly do so by making disparaging comments about the solicitor's competence or by accusing the solicitor of IRA membership. One solicitor told us that these types of remarks are made to 100% of his clients.

Interference with the Right to Counsel of Choice

- We received numerous allegations that police interrogators make derogatory comments about specific solicitors with the intention of scaring their clients away from them.

Anonymous Threats

- Several solicitors complained of anonymous threats, some in circumstances that strongly suggested collusion between members of the security forces and paramilitary groups. Others described suspected break-ins, buggings, and other forms of harassment.

Innuendo

- In Northern Ireland, officials and other public figures have too often linked lawyers with their clients' alleged causes and actions. When a lawyer receives a settlement for a client who alleges police mistreatment, some public figures recklessly speculate that such payments go to support paramilitary activities.

B. The Murder of Patrick Finucane

- The killing of Patrick Finucane in 1989 and the government's unwillingness or inability to prosecute those who are responsible continue to undermine the vitality and effectiveness of the legal profession.

- The Lawyers Committee found credible evidence that Finucane's effective legal advocacy in politically sensitive cases resulted in his harassment and ultimately led to his killing. We also found credible evidence suggesting collusion between elements within the security forces and loyalist paramilitaries in Finucane's murder.

The Army Connection

- There is substantial evidence suggesting the British Army's complicity in Finucane's murder. This link emerged during the trial of Brian Nelson. Nelson's journal links him directly to Finucane's murder.

The RUC Connection

- There is also evidence pointing to the involvement of the RUC in the form of knowing acquiescence or perhaps even instigation. Two independent sources told us that the RUC had a double agent in the Ulster Defence Association (UDA). According to these sources, the double agent informed the RUC that Finucane was a target, assuming they would prevent the murder from taking place.

The Failed Investigation

- The RUC refused to discuss any aspect of the Finucane case with us on the ground that its investigation is ongoing. Yet no one has been arrested, charged, or tried for Finucane's murder. One official told us that the killers are known and are currently serving time for other offenses. Even if true, this coincidence does not satisfy the public's need for justice or put to rest the widespread concern about official involvement in this crime.

C. General Emergency Provisions

- The legal setting in Northern Ireland all but ordains that defense lawyers suffer intimidation. Emergency provisions, coupled with practices and conditions in detention centers, give the security forces every incentive to rely on custodial interrogation as their primary method of obtaining convictions or guilty pleas. These factors make the role of legal counsel all the more crucial. They also make effective legal advocacy the subject of increased police hostility. The legal framework within which lawyers operate includes the following elements:

Detention

- Under the PTA, an individual may be held without charge for as long as seven days. These provisions stand in marked contrast to "ordinary" criminal standards. Extensions under the PTA regularly occur. In 1988, the European Court of Human Rights held that the time limits in these detention centers violated the European Convention on Human Rights. Rather than amending the law, the United Kingdom formally derogated from the Convention.

Confessions

- Just as some emergency provisions give the police the time needed to obtain confessions, others ensure that confessions and other incriminating statements are readily admissible. The current EPA standards compare unfavorably with the common law or the Police and Criminal Evidence (Northern Ireland) Order (PACE).

- The current standards of admissibility ensure that confessions remain the dominant reality of trials in the juryless, single judge Diplock courts. There is further persuasive evidence that the current standards, which by definition allow involuntary confessions, also contribute to the mistreatment of detainees.

Right to Silence

- The regular use of questionable confessions makes the effective exercise of the right to silence paramount. Recent assaults on that right make such exercise more difficult, and timely advice from counsel more crucial. Several provisions in the Criminal Evidence (Northern Ireland) Order of 1988 effectively eliminate the traditional right to silence which was previously in force. In so doing, these provisions violate international human rights protections.

D. Access to Lawyers

- Emergency provisions in Northern Ireland also subvert, rather than protect, the right to counsel. The EPA, PTA, and recent case law combine to restrict access by solicitors to their clients in both obvious and subtle ways. These include:

Delays in Access

- The law in Northern Ireland delays access to clients by a solicitor and limits the access that is given. The EPA allows police to prevent access for up to 48 hours after the initial arrest, and then for successive 48 periods. Even if access is granted, it amounts to no more than a half hour conference, after which another 48 hour denial may be authorized. Police regularly delay access under these provisions.

Judicial Review and Undertakings

- Judicial review is provided if a decision is made to deny access. However, recent legal developments have made this safeguard meaningless. A recent requirement, called an undertaking, has put lawyers in an unwarranted ethical position, which may also be dangerous. An undertaking commits a solicitor not to communicate with anyone what occurred during his or her consultation with a detained client. By definition, this practice divides the solicitor's duties between the client and the court. It compromises the solicitor's freedom to be a zealous advocate. Moreover, the RUC can challenge an undertaking simply by asserting that a solicitor is "unduly sympathetic" to a paramilitary organization. Patrick Finucane's case is a grim reminder of what such an implication may entail.

Limitations on Choice

- The EPA entitles a detainee to consult a solicitor if he or she requests. However, the RUC apparently interprets this provision to require a detainee to ask for a specific solicitor or firm. If the detainee asks a spouse or relative to contact a qualified solicitor, the police frequently bar that solicitor from the detention center because the detainee never requested that particular lawyer. Far from ensuring a meaningful choice of counsel, the RUC's practice impedes it with no evident justification.

E. Detention Practices and Conditions

• Conditions in detention centers make what appears to be a bad situation worse. These centers are central to the official campaign to garner information, informers, and confessions. As such, they are apparently designed to be coercive. They are almost completely devoid of the most basic safeguards for ensuring that abuse against detainees does not occur. Accounts from detainees are replete with stories of physical and psychological abuse. While the subject of mistreatment of detainees is beyond the scope of this report, we were encouraged to learn that they have been far fewer alleged incidents of physical mistreatment in the last year. Nonetheless, the safeguards against abuse of detainees is grossly inadequate. Among the deficiencies are these:

Lack of Monitoring of Interrogations

• Currently each detention center has closed circuit television cameras installed in interrogation rooms but not in either cells or corridors. Uniformed officers are supposed to watch to observe and report mistreatment. Yet the RUC continues to refuse to allow video or audio taping of interrogation sessions. The police argue that to do so would allow paramilitary groups to find out whether any detainee provided them with information. Like the "fear of kidnapping" justification for delaying access to solicitors, we view the police's expressed reasons for not videotaping interrogation sessions are pretextual. Few outside the RUC consider the current monitoring system effective.

Note Taking

• The RUC has recently adopted one modest reform, implementing a system for electronic timing of note taking. Electronic timing will help prevent subsequent alteration of notes, which has occurred in the past, by providing a record of when they were taken.

Lay Visitors

• For detentions under the PACE Order in Northern Ireland, a lay visitor's program has recently been introduced. Under this program, appointed members of the public visit police stations on a regular but unannounced basis.

• In December 1992, the government announced the appointment of Sir Louis Blom-Cooper QC to the newly created post of Independent Commissioner for Holding Centers. The Independent Commissioner will have authority to make unannounced visits to holding centers in order to provide an independent check that persons detained in interrogation centers on suspicion of paramilitary activity are treated fairly. The Lawyers Committee welcomes this development as a positive step and expresses its hope that the Independent Commissioner will prove effective.

F. Complaints Procedures

• An essential test for any legal system is whether there is effective accountability for violations by government agents. In this critical area, the system in Northern Ireland is failing dramatically. In cases involving suspected paramilitary activity, the RUC is accountable only unto itself. While allegations can be lodged with either the police or the Independent Commission on Police Complaints (ICPC), they can only be investigated by the police. Predictably, allegations of violations by the police are rarely prosecuted.

• Lawyers rarely lodge official complaints about police intimidation because they lack faith in complaints procedures. There are three entities, in particular, which are failing to fulfill their responsibility for addressing these complaints. They are:

<u>Royal Ulster Constabulary</u>

• There is a widely held view that in cases involving suspected paramilitary activity the RUC is virtually unaccountable to any other government entity. The RUC's record in handling complaints of harassment and intimidation of lawyers is poor. In general, there is a pervasive sentiment that the RUC lacks the will to hold its members accountable for human rights violations.

The Independent Commission on Police Complaints

- In theory, the ICPC provides an independent check on the complaints process by supervising RUC investigations of alleged police misconduct. In practice, this "safeguard" is woefully inadequate. A recent U.S. State Department report noted: "In its first 2 years of operation, the ICPC failed to substantiate any of the 840 claims of ill-treatment in police custody submitted to it."[1]

Law Society of Northern Ireland

- Few solicitors with whom we spoke have confidence in the capacity or willingness of the Law Society to effectively pursue complaints about intimidation of its members. Generally, when the Law Society has intervened in such cases, it has done so privately under the auspices of its president, usually to little or no avail.

---

[1]U.S. Department of State, *Country Reports on Human Rights Practices for 1992*, at 959 (1993).

RECOMMENDATIONS

A. Allegations of Intimidation

- There should be an independent public inquiry into allegations of official threats and abuse of defense solicitors.

- The Secretary of State for Northern Ireland should call for an official investigation into complaints of intimidation.

- Solicitors who report death threats should be accorded effective police protection.

- The Law Society of Northern Ireland should issue a public statement calling for a public inquiry into the allegations of official intimidation of defense solicitors. The Bar Council of Northern Ireland should do the same.

B. The Finucane Murder

- There should be an independent, judicial public inquiry into the murder of Patrick Finucane.

- The RUC should be required to make a public statement concerning the status of its investigation into the Finucane killing.

- The government should reprimand Douglas Hogg for his reckless statements concerning solicitors "unduly sympathetic" to paramilitary groups.

- The Law Society of Northern Ireland should issue a public statement calling for a public inquiry into the Finucane murder. The Bar Council of Northern Ireland should do the same.

C. General Emergency Provisions

Detention

- The United Kingdom should withdraw its derogation from Article 5(3) of the European Convention on Human Rights and Article 9(3) of the International Covenant on Civil and Political Rights.

- Detainees should in all cases be brought before a magistrate within 36 hours of arrest and be charged or be released within 96 hours.

Confessions

- There should be a return to the standards for admitting confessions under the Judges Rules.

Right to Silence

- The right to silence should be guaranteed. Neither courts nor juries should be permitted to draw adverse inferences from a defendant's failure to respond during police questioning or at trial.

D. Access to Lawyers

- Legal Aid for defense solicitors should be retained.

Access Restrictions

- Detainees should have immediate, regular, constant, and confidential access to solicitors of their choice.

- Detainees should have access to legal advice during interrogation as is the case for detainees under emergency legislation elsewhere in the United Kingdom.

- Solicitors should not be required to make undertakings that they will not relay communications with clients to anyone.

Choice

- Detainees should not be restricted to retaining only those solicitors of firms whom they request specifically.

E. Detention Practices and Conditions

Taping

- Interrogations should be audiotaped and videotaped.

- Solicitors who represent detainees should have access to audiotapes and videotapes of interrogations.

Lay Visitors

- A scheme should be established permitting the appointment of solicitors, barristers, magistrates, representatives from the Standing Advisory Commission on Human Rights (SACHR), and members of independent human rights organizations to visit and monitor interrogations in detention centers on a regular, unannounced basis.

F. Complaints Procedures

RUC

- Parliament should establish an investigatory force independent of the RUC, the Army, or MI5.

- The burden of proof for internal disciplinary proceedings should be a preponderance of the evidence rather than beyond a reasonable doubt.

Independent Commission on Police Complaints

- The ICPC should be given independent investigatory authority with the staff and resources sufficient for the purpose.

- The ICPC should be permitted to initiate investigations into complaints against the police.

Coroner's Inquests

- Legal Aid should be extended to Coroner's Inquests.

- Surviving family members and their solicitors should have the power to conduct discovery in connection with Coroner's Inquests.

- Members of the security forces should be subject to a summons to give testimony under oath subject to questioning during the Coroner's inquest on the same basis as any other witness.

- The Coroner should exercise discretion to hear evidence bearing on possible involvement of the security forces in suspicious deaths. The mandate of the Coroner should also be expanded to make exclusion of such evidence impossible.

Law Society

- The Law Society should establish formal public complaints procedures for solicitors alleging official harassment or threats.

INTRODUCTION

For almost a quarter century residents of Northern Ireland have lived with a jarring combination of normalcy and upheaval. Patrols armed with semiautomatic weapons share the same streets with children and commuters. Busy pubs and theaters coexist with bombings and sectarian killings. Full court calendars attest to the rule of law despite repeated adjudications of international human rights violations.[2] When the Lawyers Committee mission arrived in Northern Ireland in late August of 1992, the region reached the grim milestone of 3,000 deaths since the outbreak of the "Troubles" in 1969.[3] Northern Ireland's singularity, however, goes well beyond even the strife of the last quarter century. From its inception in 1922, Northern Ireland has lived under emergency legislation that has afforded the police extraordinary powers at the expense of individual freedoms. This historic legal setting, combined with the ongoing sectarian conflict, renders the position of defense lawyers at once critical and fraught with peril.

A. Background

Northern Ireland was born out of the same conflict that produced what is now the Irish Republic. Following the First World War, a guerrilla campaign led by the Irish Republican Army (IRA) led the United Kingdom Parliament to conclude that autonomy for Ireland was in Great Britain's best interest. The Protestant minority resisted Irish autonomy with threats of force. The solution became a partition of the island into two parts. Twenty-six counties were granted effective independence in the form of dominion status within the British

---

[2]*See, e.g., Ireland v. United Kingdom* (1978) (certain forms of interrogation held to be inhuman and degrading treatment under the European Convention on Human Rights); *Brogan v. United Kingdom* (1987) (detention for more than four days without judicial authorization held to violate the European Convention on Human Rights). *See generally*, Helsinki Watch, *Human Rights in Northern Ireland* (1991) [hereinafter Helsinki Watch Report]; William E. Hellerstein, Robert B. McKay, Peter R. Schlam, *Criminal Justice and Human Rights in Northern Ireland, A Report to the Association of the Bar of the City of New York* (1988) [hereinafter NYC Bar Report].

[3]*Irish Times*, Aug. 28, 1992, at 10-11.

Commonwealth as the Irish Free State. Overwhelmingly Catholic and officially committed to the revival of the Irish language and the island's Celtic heritage, this state adopted a new constitution in 1937 and subsequently left the British Commonwealth, becoming the Republic of Ireland. The six remaining counties, part of the historic northern province of Ulster, were established as a self-governing unit within the United Kingdom. The new area of Northern Ireland was populated by a Protestant majority that could trace its origins to seventeenth-century Scottish and English settlements. This majority was firmly committed to maintaining its link to Britain. A significant Catholic minority was for the most part dissatisfied with separation from the rest of Ireland.[4]

The basic post-World War I demographic patterns hold, but significant shifts have recently occurred. For decades the population in Northern Ireland maintained a ratio of about two-thirds Protestant and one-third Catholic. Unofficial reports of the latest census figures, taken in 1991, indicate that today roughly 57% of the populace is Protestant, mainly Presbyterian, and 43% is Roman Catholic.[5] The total population of the six counties remains about 1.5 million. Most Protestants are unionists, so-called for wanting to preserve the union with the United Kingdom. Most Catholics remain nationalists committed to making Northern Ireland part of the Irish Republic. Extreme unionists, especially those who advocate violence, are generally called loyalists. Their extreme nationalist counterparts are usually referred to as republicans.

The Northern Ireland Parliament began operation in 1922, eventually going by the name "Stormont" after the massive parliament building it came to occupy in Belfast. For 50 years Stormont exercised jurisdiction over most governmental functions except for taxation and defense. The organic act creating the Stormont government could have afforded protection of minority rights in Northern Ireland by binding safeguards enforced by a judiciary exercising judicial review over local legislation. That course was not followed. With uncontrolled majority power, the Stormont regime consistently pursued discriminatory policies

---

[4]*See* R.F. Foster, *Modern Ireland, 1600-1972*, at 582-92 (1988).

[5]*Sunday Independent*, Nov. 1, 1992, at 1.

against Catholics in employment, housing, and voting rights. Confronted with this situation, much of the Catholic populace either could not or would not participate in Northern Ireland's governance. Many also asserted a desire to be part of a united Ireland. Some of the minority population pursued this last goal by engaging in sporadic paramilitary activity conducted by the IRA.

During the late 1960s, many Catholics had begun to take part in peaceful civil rights demonstrations modeled after the African-American civil rights movement in the United States. The unionist response was often derisive and at times violent. Majority violence encouraged some in the minority to turn away from peaceful protest to participation in IRA paramilitary activities. A dormant IRA resurfaced, eventually splitting into its "Official" and more active and lethal "Provisional" wings. Loyalist paramilitary groups in turn reappeared, including the Ulster Volunteer Force (UVF) and the Ulster Defence Association (UDA). British troops were deployed to Northern Ireland to respond to the situation in August 1969, and have remained ever since.

The violence peaked in 1972 with 467 political fatalities. Since then, the number of political killings per year has fallen but remains high, ranging from a low of 54 to a high of 97 in the last decade. Likewise, the number of injuries related to the security situation during the same period has averaged 450 per year.[6] Of the 3,000 deaths in Northern Ireland's violence from 1969 though August 28, 1992: 33% consisted of Catholic civilians; 31%, members of the security forces; 21%, Protestant civilians; 10%, republican paramilitaries; and 3%, loyalist paramilitaries.[7] Officials of the Royal Ulster Constabulary (RUC), Northern Ireland's police force, told our delegation that they expected the present level of violence to continue for the next 10 to 15 years, due largely to major arms shipments to the IRA from overseas.

The numerical strength of the security forces has, moreover, increased in recent years. Currently the ranks of the RUC stand at about

---

[6]Royal Ulster Constabulary, "Statistical Information," at 2 (1992).

[7]Two percent fell into the category "others." *Irish Times*, Aug. 28, 1992, at 10.

8,500, with about 4,500 in the full or part-time reserve.[8] Troops number about 18,500, 12,500 in the regular British Army and 6,000 in the newly constituted Royal Irish Regiment (RIR), the successor to the locally recruited Ulster Defence Regiment (UDR).[9]

B. Statutory Framework

In 1972, the same year the death toll reached 467, the British Parliament suspended Stormont, abolishing it one year later. The resulting system of direct rule, though originally intended to be temporary, remains the framework under which Northern Ireland is governed. Under the 1973 Northern Ireland Constitution Act and 1974 Northern Ireland Act -- as amended by the 1979 House of Commons Redistribution of Seats Act -- Northern Ireland holds 17 seats in the Parliament in Westminster. Legislation over most matters takes the form of Orders in Council, which are submitted for approval by the Commons and Lords and then referred to the Queen in the Privy Council for approval. Parliament also retains its ultimate authority to enact statutes binding Northern Ireland directly.

Executive authority also remains in Westminster in the person of the Secretary of State for Northern Ireland. Invariably a Member of Parliament for an English district, this official serves in the British Cabinet and manages the Northern Ireland Office (NIO). The NIO consults on security matters with both the RUC and the Army, but becomes directly involved only when police or army operations touch upon a matter of general public interest. Thus, the Secretary of State for Northern Ireland is responsible for security policy, while the Chief Constable of the RUC takes the lead in security operations. By statute, however, the RUC is answerable only to the law and the courts, not to the government. The Army, which functions under the direction of the police in a back-up capacity, serves under the local commanding general, who reports to the Chief of the General Staff in Great Britain. The

---

[8]Royal Ulster Constabulary, "Chief Constable's Report, 1991," at 66 (1992).

[9]*Financial Times*, Sept. 21, 1992, at 14.

Chief of the General Staff in Great Britain in turn reports to the Secretary of State for Defence, an elected politician.[10]

Two measures frame the government's response to political violence. Both are also direct Acts of Parliament. The first is the Northern Ireland (Emergency Provisions) Act 1991 (EPA), which follows the lines of early Emergency Provisions Acts enacted in 1973, 1975, 1978, and 1987. The second is the Prevention of Terrorism (Temporary Provisions) Act 1989 (PTA), which follows the lines of earlier Prevention of Terrorism Acts enacted in 1974, 1976, and 1984. While the EPA applies only to Northern Ireland, the PTA operates throughout the United Kingdom. Together the EPA and PTA establish a system designed to garner convictions based on readily admissible confessions obtained through extended periods of detention and interrogation. To preserve this system, the United Kingdom has been forced to derogate from international human rights undertakings on numerous occasions.[11]

Emergency legislation has been a feature of Northern Ireland since its creation. Such legislation began with the Civil Authorities (Special Powers) Act (Northern Ireland), which itself replaced the Restoration of Order in Ireland Act (1920). Originally conceived as a temporary measure, the Special Powers Act became a permanent feature on the legal landscape in 1933. With the outbreak of sustained violence, the Special Powers Act was invoked to introduce a policy of internment

---

[10]Lawyers Committee interview of John Ledlie, Nicholas Perry, David Lavery, David McIroy at the Northern Ireland Office, Sept. 3, 1992.

[11]The United Kingdom entered derogations under the International Covenant on Civil and Political Rights (ICCPR) on December 23, 1988 and on May 17, 1976. It has also derogated from the European Convention on Human Rights on December 23, 1988; December 18, 1978; December 12, 1975; September 19, 1975; August 16, 1973; January 23, 1973; August 20, 1971; September 25, 1969; and June 27, 1957. For adjudications of human rights violations, *see supra*, note 2. Currently, the U.K. maintains only its December 23, 1988 derogations from Article 5(3) of the European Convention and Article 9(3) of the ICCPR, each of which concerns detention.

-- indefinite detention without trial -- in 1971. This extreme step led to a review of criminal justice in Northern Ireland by a commission chaired by Lord Diplock.[12]

The recommendations of the Diplock Commission led directly to the repeal of the Special Powers Act and the passage of the EPA. The EPA retained many features of the Special Powers Act, including the power of internment which remains on the books to this day. The EPA also led to the eventual phasing out of internment in practice by establishing the so-called "Diplock Courts" in which certain "scheduled" offenses often but not exclusively associated with political violence are tried without a jury by a single judge. Aside from reserving the power of internment, the EPA empowers the police to stop and question individuals regarding identity and recent movements and further authorizes the search of persons and residences, as well as examination and seizure of documents, all without prior judicial approval.

Parliament passed the PTA in 1974 in response to the killing of 21 people in two bomb attacks in Birmingham. Though intended to expire after six months, the PTA endures. Features of the PTA currently enable the authorities to proscribe paramilitary organizations and make membership in them illegal; to issue orders excluding citizens of the United Kingdom from Northern Ireland, England and Wales, or Scotland without trial or judicial review; and to arrest, detain, and interrogate individuals for up to seven days without an appearance before a magistrate.

One further relevant measure is the 1989 Police and Criminal Evidence (Northern Ireland) Order (PACE), which to a great extent tracks the 1984 Police and Criminal Evidence Act governing England and Wales. The PACE Order in general applies to non-scheduled

---

[12]Subsequent government commissions have periodically reported on the security and criminal justice systems. In 1975, a commission headed by Lord Gardiner recommended that internment without trial should not remain as a long term policy. In 1978, a committee of inquiry headed by Judge Bennett reviewed interrogation practices amidst allegations of inhuman and degrading treatment. In 1984, Judge Baker issued recommendations that served as the basis for the 1987 EPA. Since 1986, Lord Colville has prepared annual reports on security matters.

offenses and provides greater protection of individual rights than either the EPA or PTA.

C. The Role of Lawyers

The United Nations Basic Principles on the Role of Lawyers[13] accord practitioners several guarantees for their work and safety. These include:

> 1. All persons are entitled to call upon the assistance of a lawyer of their choice to protect and establish their rights to defend them in all stages of criminal proceedings.
>
> * * *
>
> 8. All arrested, detained or imprisoned persons shall be provided with adequate opportunities, time and facilities to be visited by and to communicate and consult with a lawyer, without delay, interception or censorship and in full confidentiality. Such consultations may be within sight, but not within the hearing, of law enforcement officials.
>
> * * *
>
> 16. Governments shall ensure that lawyers (a) are able to perform all their professional functions without intimidation, hinderance, harassment or improper interference; (b) are able to travel and consult with their clients freely both within their country and abroad; and (c) shall not suffer, or be threatened with, prosecution or administrative, economic or other sanctions for any

[13]These principles were adopted by the Eighth United Nations Conference on the Prevention of Crime and the Treatment of Offenders in August and September 1990. The UN General Assembly "welcomed" the instruments in resolutions 45/121, December 14, 1990, and 45/166, December 18, 1990.

action taken in accordance with recognized professional duties, standards and ethics.

> 17. Where the security of lawyers is threatened as a result of discharging their functions, they shall be adequately safeguarded by the authorities.

> 18. Lawyers shall not be identified with their clients or their clients' causes as a result of discharging their functions.

* * *

Similarly, the European Committee for the Prevention of Torture has stated:

> As regards more particularly the right of access to legal advice, it is important for police officers to refrain from discouraging in any way the exercise of this right by detainees.[14]

Even when described in bare outline, the situation in Northern Ireland suggests that defense lawyers must play a crucial and hazardous role. The abrogation of certain rights makes the involvement of counsel essential for the protection of those rights that remain. The UN Basic Principles and other international human rights agreements recognize that the rule of law can survive only if an independent bar is allowed to zealously defend clients regardless of the gravity of the charge. The U.K. government in part recognizes this principle as well, as witness its laudable scheme of legal aid payments to solicitors who practice in the criminal courts. Yet the enhanced importance of lawyers is also precisely what places them in greater jeopardy. The thrust of Northern Ireland's emergency legislation makes any stumbling block to obtaining convictions suspect. The emotions fired by the killing of police and soldiers can only add to such resentment. In this atmosphere, it is not surprising that the fundamental distinction between lawyer and client is too often lost.

---

[14]Council of Europe, CPT/Inf(91)15, para. 218.

In its response to a draft of this report, the Northern Ireland Office pointed out to us that statistically "the position of defense lawyers is less hazardous than being, for example, a member of the judiciary, a member of the security forces, or a member of other occupations in Northern Ireland." (See Appendix A.) It made the further point that judges, magistrates, and prosecution lawyers have also been murdered. Deputy Chief Constable Michael McAtamney made the same point on behalf of the RUC. (See Appendix B.) We acknowledge as much. The international human rights community, however, can be confident that any state, including the United Kingdom, will without any involvement from that community, do all that can be done to protect those through whom it exercises its sanctioning powers. Our concern obviously must be for those against whom those powers are directed, and the lawyers who represent them.

The killing of Patrick Finucane, a leader among Northern Ireland's defense solicitors, remains the most extreme example of the risks lawyers in the region face. Finucane was murdered on February 12, 1989 when a group of masked gunmen shot him in his home while he and his family were having Sunday dinner. The Ulster Freedom Fighters (UFF) subsequently claimed responsibility for the killing, but to date no one has been arrested for the crime. Finucane was and is the only practicing defense lawyer murdered in Northern Ireland. Though unique, his case also illustrates many of the problems his colleagues continue to face and still commands local and international attention.

Official observers and non-governmental organizations have expressed serious concerns about the Finucane case, allegations of threats directed at Northern Ireland defense lawyers, and human rights conditions in Northern Ireland generally. A partial list includes: Claire Palley, the independent expert nominated by the U.K. government to the United Nations Sub-Commission on the Prevention of Discrimination and the Protection of Minorities; Louis Joinet, author of a report on the independence of the judiciary and the protection of practicing lawyers for the same sub-commission; Peter Burns, Rapporteur on the United Kingdom for the (UN) Committee Against Torture; the Northern Ireland Standing Advisory Commission on Human Rights (SACHR); Viscount Colville of Culross QC; Amnesty International; the International Federation of Human Rights; the Committee on the Administration of

Justice; Liberty; British Irish Rights Watch; the Haldane Society; Helsinki Watch; and the Association of the Bar of the City of New York. This report seeks to augment, update, and integrate the work of these and other groups and individuals.[15]

Part I of this study explores the evidence indicating that intimidation of defense lawyers is widespread. Interviews with solicitors and their clients reveal that nearly every lawyer with whom we spoke who engages in representation of defendants charged under the emergency legislation is the target of remarks by RUC interrogators made in detention centers. These remarks, in intent and effect, scare off potential clients, drive a wedge between clients and solicitors already retained, and directly threaten the solicitors themselves. We also found evidence of the harassment of solicitors which, though indirect, appears to have originated in official quarters. Finally, we conclude that the official and unofficial procedures for complaints against the security forces are well intended but woefully inadequate.

Part II addresses troubling and persistent questions about the Finucane killing that have yet to be put to rest. We conclude that Finucane was an able and inventive lawyer, who was among a handful of solicitors whose successful and legitimate advocacy for clients went beyond standard criminal defense. The evidence we gathered further suggests that Finucane's very success subjected him to various forms of official intimidation prior to his murder. There is additional evidence pointing to collusion between the UFF and the security forces in the murder itself. To date, we conclude, official responses have been inadequate both in execution and results. For these reasons, the Lawyers Committee agrees with Claire Palley, who in official remarks before the UN Sub-Commission on the Prevention of Discrimination and the Protection of Minorities, stated that the U.K. government should "set up an independent public inquiry into the death of Mr. Finucane." As she

---

[15]Specific citations to reports, studies, or remarks will be made where appropriate.

noted, "[s]uspicions of official collusion in Mr. Finucane's murder must be put at rest."[16]

Part III turns to the legal setting that not only allows but apparently encourages the types of abuses alleged. First, it examines those features of legislation and case law that ensure a setting for intimidation, including prolonged detention, a lower standard for admitting confessions into evidence, and the diminution of the right to silence. Next, it explores the practices and physical conditions under which interrogations take place. This section then looks in detail at the rules governing access to lawyers specifically. Lastly, we consider the complaints procedures available to solicitors subject to harassment. In light of the legal framework in which defense lawyers in Northern Ireland practice, we concur in the observation of Louis Joinet in his 1992 report to the UN Sub-Commission on Prevention of Discrimination and Protection of Minorities that the United Kingdom's obligation to adhere to international standards concerning lawyers is "all the more necessary when lawyers as a result of discharging their functions are identified with their clients or their clients' causes."[17]

When appropriate, established or potential violations of international human rights standards are noted throughout.

---

[16]Remarks of Dr. Claire Palley, UN Sub-Commission on the Prevention of Discrimination Against Minorities, Aug. 19, 1992. Dr. Palley's comments echoed similar concerns voiced by, among other groups, Amnesty International. Amnesty International, *United Kingdom: Human Rights Concerns*, at 56 (June 1991).

[17]Louis Joinet, *The Independence and Impartiality of the Judiciary, Jurors and Assessors and the Independence of Lawyers*, UN Sub-Commission on Prevention of Discrimination and Protection of Minorities, 44th Session, UN Doc. E/CN.4/Sub.2/1992/25, at 23 (Aug. 5, 1992).

I. INTIMIDATION OF LAWYERS

During the evening of Sunday, February 12, 1989, Patrick Finucane, a 38-year-old Belfast solicitor; his wife, Geraldine; and his three children aged 9, 13, and 17 were eating dinner and watching television in the kitchen of their home in North Belfast.[18] At approximately 7:25 p.m., a loud noise came from the front door. Finucane and his wife jumped up from the table, and Finucane opened the glass fire door leading to the front hall. Halfway down the hall two masked figures dressed in black with camouflage jackets advanced with drawn pistols. Mrs. Finucane, who was standing just behind her husband, attempted to activate a panic alarm behind the kitchen door. According to Finucane's eldest son, his father's last act was to throw himself up against the door.[19] Two or three shots shattered the glass and hit Finucane in the chest and stomach, leaving him lying face up on the floor. The gunmen entered the kitchen and shot Finucane in the head and neck about a dozen more times, at least once and probably more from a range of about 15 inches. At some point Mrs. Finucane was herself wounded in the ankle, probably by a ricocheting bullet. The children were unharmed physically but witnessed everything.

The police and neighbors arrived within minutes of the shooting, but by this time Finucane had already died. The autopsy showed that Finucane had been struck 12 times by a 9mm Browning automatic and twice by a .38 Special Revolver. It would turn out later that the Browning was one of 13 stolen from Palace Army Barracks by a member of the Ulster Defence Regiment (UDR) who was later convicted for the theft.

---

[18] Unless otherwise indicated, this account is based on depositions taken at the Coroner's Inquest, Sept. 1990.

[19] Michael J. Graham, "Report on the Assassination of Patrick Finucane," at 7 (1989). Graham is a U.S. attorney who wrote a report on the murder in order to persuade the National Lawyers Guild to sponsor an inquiry. His report includes an account of the murder as witnessed by Finucane's eldest son.

The next day, Monday, February 13, 1989, a male caller telephoned the press with the statement: "The UFF [Ulster Freedom Fighters] claim responsibility for the execution of Pat Finucane, the PIRA [Provisional Irish Republican Army] Officer, not the solicitor. While Provos continue to execute Loyalists, and members of the security forces who share their lunch with them then there will be inevitable retaliation." At the Coroner's Inquest, Detective Superintendent Simpson rejected out of hand the UFF's allegation, stating that "the Police refute the claim that Mr Finucane was a member of the PIRA. He was just another law-abiding citizen going about his professional duties in a professional manner."

Numerous detainees, solicitors, and journalists told the Lawyers Committee mission that the security forces in Northern Ireland violate basic international standards safeguarding the role of lawyers on a regular and ongoing basis. Credible evidence suggests that Patrick Finucane's murder was simply the most heinous instance of systematic harassment of defense lawyers simply for doing their job. Nor does any end appear in sight without significant reforms.

A. Legal Defense in Northern Ireland

The Northern Ireland legal community that specializes in defense work is small and vulnerable. It is as an initial matter divided between solicitors and barristers. Detainees deal in the first instance with solicitors, and it is they who appear to bear the brunt of official hostility. Solicitors have the duties of advising clients against self-incrimination, protecting them against ill-treatment, and investigating for exculpatory evidence. These responsibilities constantly bring solicitors into contact with police officers and place them in the path of police investigations.

Few solicitors choose to take on these duties. Northern Ireland has about 1,400 solicitors. Of these only a minuscule proportion regularly engages in criminal defense work, whether scheduled offenses or "regular" criminal matters. Fewer still move beyond defense work to pursue claims for police mistreatment, habeas corpus petitions, or the other types of impact litigation for which Patrick Finucane became known.

The decentralization of the legal profession adds to the difficulties that defense lawyers face. Other features of this group augment its difficulties. Few solicitor's firms in Northern Ireland exceed three or four partners. This means that defense practitioners are spread out among seven or eight firms, none of which are in close contact. Sharing information, sharing concerns, and providing mutual assistance usually remain hopes rather than realities.

In one regard Northern Ireland defense lawyers are well off, especially compared to many of their counterparts in the United States. Potential clients in Northern Ireland may retain any solicitor they chose, and the government-funded legal aid scheme will pay for those services without any contributions being required by the client. Yet even this progressive system is not without drawbacks. Several solicitors told our delegation that the scheme provokes unjustifiable resentment among the police and even among civil solicitors who do not do criminal work. Such a response is troubling, particularly given the dangers defense solicitors face. More troubling, however, is the possibility that the government may reduce or eliminate legal aid. It would be ironic in the extreme if, of numerous possible reform measures that the government could adopt, it were to decide on attacking one of the more admirable features of a criminal justice system that is otherwise often and justly condemned.[20]

B. Harassment of Lawyers in Detention Centers

Most allegations of lawyer abuse focus on activity said to occur in detention centers. Such centers have been set up in Castlereagh (Belfast), Gough Barracks (Armagh), and Strand Road, (London/Derry[21]). In the typical story, detectives conducting "interviews" will bully and threaten the detainee, and make bullying and threatening remarks about the solicitor the detainee has requested. Some

---

[20]Lawyers Committee interviews of Peter Madden, Aug. 24 & 30, 1992; Padraigin Drinan, Aug. 30, 1992; Barra McGrory; Sept. 1, 1992.

[21]Unionists call the city Londonderry; nationalists call it Derry. Following the convention used by Helsinki Watch, we refer to it as London/Derry. *See* Helsinki Watch Report, *supra* note 2, at 5 note 7.

comments amount to outright threats. Others interfere with the attorney/client relationship. Still others interfere with a detainee's right to counsel of one's choice.

Death Threats. The most serious allegations of "intimidation, hinderance, [and] harassment" of lawyers involve death threats. Clients report that police interrogators frequently threaten the lives of their solicitors. Solicitors who once considered such threats as no more than improper interrogation devices take them much more seriously since Patrick Finucane's murder. This concern applies with special force to the apparently numerous threats that make gleeful reference to Finucane's death.

Almost every solicitor the Lawyers Committee mission interviewed related stories of death threats. An especially sobering account came from Barra McGrory. McGrory stated that in two recent instances clients who told him that both he and they had been threatened were later shot dead. One was Conor McGuire, who had been involved with the Irish National Liberation Army (INLA), a republican paramilitary group. Around February 1992, McGuire, released from detention in Castlereagh, told McGrory not to park his car near the detention center. McGuire said that the interrogators told him that, "the police were going to kill me and they're gonna stiff you, too."[22] A week later McGuire was dead at the hands of loyalists. In a letter to the Chief Constable, McGrory wrote, "threats about my own personal safety are frequently passed on by clients following the interview in Castlereagh. On this occasion however I have the uncomfortable experience of knowing that my client who claimed to have been threatened in a similar manner has now been killed."[23] The other incident involved Martin O'Prey. O'Prey, who was regularly detained in Castlereagh, told McGrory that the police told him that both he and "that wee shit McGrory" would be killed. O'Prey was also murdered.[24]

---

[22]*Andersonstown News*, Mar. 11, 1992, at 17.

[23]Letter dated May 6, 1992 from Barra McGrory to Chief Constable Hugh Annesley.

[24]Lawyers Committee interview of Barra McGrory, Sept. 1, 1992.

Other solicitors echoed McGrory's concerns. P.J. McGrory, Peter Madden, and Phillip Breen all asserted that death threats made in detention centers amount to an occupational hazard. Joseph Rice stated that there is no doubt that if a solicitor rocks the boat too much, like Patrick Finucane, he or she will be in trouble.[25] There was some disagreement as to when threats became a problem, some asserting the practice went back 20 years while others said only five or ten. All agreed, however, that the problem persists.

Clients confirmed the threats. One recent detainee, Geraldine O'Connor, related a typical allegation. On July 21, 1991, she was detained under Section 14 of the PTA and asked for Madden & Finucane as counsel. One of the interrogators replied, "[s]he's a member of PIRA and who does she ask for? Another Provie." Later during the interrogation the detectives said that Patrick Finucane had ended up in a body bag and that Kevin Winters, another solicitor at Madden & Finucane, "would end up the same way."[26]

Nearly every detainee the Lawyers Committee mission interviewed had similar stories. Another Madden & Finucane client, John Pierce, spoke of a detention in November 1990. During the interrogation, detectives made several remarks about Winters, who was Pierce's solicitor. These included: "your solicitor is an up and coming problem"; "Kevin Winters is not such a problem that it can't be sorted out like Pat Finucane"; and "should he [Winters] rise above himself we'll leave him with his fucking mate." Pierce added that no death threats against Winters were made during a more recent detention, this one in August 1992, but that the police continued to refer to his solicitor as "that fucking Kevin Winters."[27] Other detainees describe comparable recent death threats against Peter Madden.[28]

---

[25]Lawyers Committee interview of Joseph Rice, Sept. 3, 1992.

[26]Lawyers Committee interview of Geraldine O'Connor, Sept. 3, 1992.

[27]Lawyers Committee interview of John Pierce, Sept. 3, 1992.

[28]Lawyers Committee interviews of Brian Austin and Patrick McDade, Aug. 31, 1992.

Madden & Finucane in the regular course of its representation records instructions taken from clients held in detention. These records corroborate the allegations made by its clients to the Lawyers Committee delegation. A sampling of recorded threatening remarks includes:

- "They were also abusive about my solicitor. . . . They said he was a murderer and that they would stiff him."

- "They referred to my solicitor . . . and referred to him as 'a dirty provo scumbag and that he should be getting the same as Pat.'"

- "Asked for solicitor . . . CID [the Criminal Investigation Division] said, 'Finucane is dead, anyone you get in contact with is dead as well.'"

- "We have got him [the solicitor] down in our wee red book. All he is is a Provo with qualifications. Said he was just an IRA man like that bastard Finucane and will end up the same way."[29]

Interference with the Attorney/Client Relationship. Another set of allegations involve attempts to drive a wedge between clients and solicitors. These attempts take the form of comments ranging from slanders against the solicitor's competence to accusations of membership in the IRA. While less serious than death threats, sources we interviewed agreed that comments aimed at denigrating solicitors were more common. Patrick Fahy, a solicitor from Omagh, reported that these types of remarks were made to "100%" of his clients and often "became so bad as to be unbelievable." Fahy said that interrogators invariably told his clients that he was a "Provo bastard," or a "smart terrorist."[30] Each of the solicitors we spoke with echoed Fahy's sentiments. Barra McGrory pointed to similar comments, as when one constable told a client, "McGrory is an IRA brief." Peter Madden noted

---

[29]Records of instructions from clients, Madden & Finucane [hereinafter Madden & Finucane Records].

[30]Lawyers Committee interview of Patrick Fahy, Sept. 1, 1992.

other forms of abuse as well. These include remarks like, "your solicitor doesn't care about you" and "he's only making money off of you." Several solicitors said that the interrogators would also make at times bizarre remarks about their personal habits, including accusations that they were sleeping with a given client's wife or girlfriend.

Many solicitors told our delegation that this kind of abuse is so routine that many clients simply do not pass it along. Those who do, however, confirm what the solicitors assert. John Pierce spoke of remarks during a detention as recent as August 18, 1992. When he was visited by Phillip Breen rather than Kevin Winters, the interrogators chided him that "Kevin Winters doesn't care about you" and "looks like Winters has forgotten where his Legal Aid money is coming from." Geraldine O'Connor said that during her June 1991 detention, the detective told her solicitors Kevin Winters and Phillip Breen were, "all provies under the belt;" that they did not care about her, and that they were only in it "for the Legal Aid money." Patrick Malloy added that when he was detained in 1989, just after Patrick Finucane's murder, the police said to him, "now Peter Madden would have to be sworn," meaning that with Finucane gone Madden would be taking his place as an IRA operative.

Madden & Finucane's business records of instructions from clients echo the preceding accounts. Typical remarks include:

- "They said my solicitor was giving me bad advice and that he was just a wanker."

- "They told me I had a bad solicitor and suggested I got rid of him."

- "They said the solicitor wasn't interested or worried about me and that all he was interested in was getting well paid for coming up and seeing me."

- "They said that the solicitor was an IRA man in a suit, another provie on their payroll, the solicitor didn't give a damn about me."[31]

Interference with the Right to Counsel of Choice. Still another type of purported police misconduct violates what the UN Basic Principles describe as the right of all persons "to call upon the assistance of a lawyer of their choice." We heard numerous allegations that the same type of derogatory remarks aimed at interfering with the attorney/client relationship are also used to scare clients away from certain solicitors in the first place.

Barra McGrory noted that the police in Castlereagh will tell first time detainees who ask for his firm, "what do you want them for? They're IRA lawyers." Other solicitors stressed this point as well. Padraigin Drinan, for example, stated that several of her clients have told her that it is commonplace for the police to state, "if you pick Madden & Finucane, then you must be in the IRA." The solicitors also pointed out that such remarks can scare off potential Protestant clients in particular, especially those involved in "quasi-criminal" activity like traffic violations. Patrick Fahy related at least one instance in which a potential client, a Protestant who had been charged with non-political criminal activity, was scared off. When he asked for Fahy the police rebuked him for requesting "a murdering Provo bastard." The defendant then chose another solicitor and was convicted.

C. Other Harassment Against Lawyers

No solicitor mentioned that he or she had ever been threatened face to face by members of the security forces. Several, however, complained of anonymous threats, some in circumstances that strongly suggested collusion between members of the security forces and paramilitary groups. Still others voiced suspicion of bugging, break-ins, and other forms of harassment.

Anonymous Threats. One particularly suggestive threat arose in connection with an official grievance that one lawyer lodged with the

---

[31]Madden & Finucane Records, *supra* note 29.

RUC, which was in turn supervised by the Independent Commission of Police Complaints (ICPC or Commission).[32] According to the lawyer, the grievance alleged that several RUC officers had taken a client to a loyalist meeting house and then to a field to be shot. The client escaped and told his lawyer what had taken place. In response to the lawyer's complaint, an investigating detective from the RUC responded that the client's story was not possible and that the complaint should be withdrawn. Two days later, the lawyer's spouse phoned the lawyer to say that someone had been calling their home wanting to discuss the case. Eventually the caller said to pass along the message that, "there will be a visit from the UFF if the complaint is not dropped." This occurred less than six months after the Finucane killing.

Another lawyer related stories of anonymous death threats as well. Padraigin Drinan, who is not known as a specialist in criminal cases, stated that she received repeated threats from the UDA in connection with her representation of two women raped by a UDA member. Among the individuals whom the police suspected to be behind the threats was a certain named individual. Sometime later, when Drinan went to see another client in prison concerning a prisoners' rights case, a paper was on the table of the visiting room with the single word -- the last name of the individual thought to be behind the earlier death threats.[33]

Patrick Fahy also gave accounts of death threats, though these lacked any obvious connection to the security forces. One took place in 1987 around the time the Irish National Liberation Army (INLA) murdered the unionist politician George Seawright. Not long afterward someone called Fahy's home and told his then-fiancee, "Do you know George Seawright? Tell Fahy that he's next." Eleven years previously, in 1976, Fahy received a box of bullets sent anonymously, a package that the solicitor considered a clear threat against his life.[34]

---

[32]For the role of the ICPC, *see infra* pages 38-40, 87-88.

[33]Lawyers Committee interview of Padraigin Drinan, Aug. 30, 1992.

[34]Lawyers Committee interview of Patrick Fahy, Sept. 1, 1992.

Harassment. In addition, solicitors relayed miscellaneous abuse ranging from specific incidents to general suspicions. Drinan told of one occurrence when she was stopped at a police checkpoint and refused to let the authorities see what was in the files she had on the back seat of her car. She was detained and questioned for four hours under the PTA and photographed while in custody. The police also rummaged through her files, only to find that they contained nothing more than conveyancing records.

Fears of bugging and other forms of surveillance are also common. Peter Madden said that the members of his firm operate on the assumption that their phones are tapped. Another solicitor alleged consistent tampering with office files, from having those files rearranged to having them stolen. This solicitor claimed to have reason to suspect the involvement of the security forces, but would not go into detail on the record for fear of retaliation.

D. Innuendo

In Northern Ireland today, to invert the words of the UN Basic Principles, too many persons serving in official capacities appear to regularly "identi[fy lawyers] with their clients or their clients' causes as a result of discharging their functions." As distressing as this perception may be, more distressing are official efforts which contribute to it.

Compensation Payments. Nowhere do such efforts raise more serious concern than with regard to settlements that solicitors secure for clients who file claims against the police for mistreatment. In at least two instances, public figures have recklessly speculated that such payments go into terrorist coffers.

Ken Maginnis is an Ulster Unionist MP, parliamentary adviser to the Northern Ireland Police Federation, and a prominent politician with close ties to the police. On December 17, 1991, Maginnis submitted a written parliamentary question to the Northern Ireland Secretary, asking the extent of compensation settlements paid out to Madden & Finucane clients since June 1989 and how many of the complaints had been substantiated by the ICPC. The Secretary replied that the information was unavailable in the form requested. The next day, Maginnis stated on a BBC radio program:

> . . . We've got to the stage where our Government is actually helping to finance terrorism. Now I don't know whether people know that. But we've just paid out to one solicitors firm alone £134,000 to 59 people who were questioned in Castlereagh holding station.

Maginnis did not name Madden & Finucane, but the figures were nearly identical to information that the firm had the previous month submitted to the (UN) Committee Against Torture. Maginnis did, however, single out Madden & Finucane by name subsequently. One of his most recent statements came during a parliamentary debate in June 1992. There, speaking under parliamentary privilege and so immune from civil action, he stated:

> The Government fall down, as it were, when it comes to claims against the Royal Ulster Constabulary that are made by those taken in for interrogation. On being released, there are claims of ill-treatment, which constitute a real money spinner. We reached the stage when a firm of solicitors, Madden & Finucane, to which I have referred in the House before, is able to boast on behalf of its clients the vast sums that it has obtained in compensation from the Northern Ireland Office without ever having to go to court.

Given the atmosphere before the Finucane murder and the tensions that followed, the Maginnis statements are irresponsible. Maginnis' political views may make his comments comprehensible, but not defensible.[35]

---

[35]British Irish Rights Watch, *Intimidation of Defence Lawyers in Northern Ireland*, at 7-9 (1992) [hereinafter *Intimidation of Defence Lawyers*] ; British Irish Rights Watch, *Intimidation of Defence Lawyers in Northern Ireland: Update*, at 2 (1992) [hereinafter *Intimidation of Defence Lawyers Update*].

Since 1986, Lord Colville has been the government-appointed reviewer responsible for drafting ostensibly independent assessments of the security situation in Northern Ireland. In his *Report on the Operation in 1991 of the Prevention of Terrorism (Temporary Provisions) Act of 1989*, he wrote:

> 6.3 . . . [T]here is some danger that hundreds of thousands of pounds overall will be paid out without any actions being tried. I have no evidence who are the plaintiffs, but if they are connected with any terrorist organizations, I would be bound to contemplate into what bank account the settlement money would go.
>
> 6.4 The result of all this is disturbing:
>
> 6.4.1 if the police are settling these cases, they are admitting ill-treatment of detainees;
> 6.4.2 in that most cases officers may not be disciplined for assault; but in most cases because the complainant will not pursue the matter in a forum where the criminal burden of proof must be used, or not at all;
> 6.4.3 in either event grave doubts are shed upon the integrity of the police;
> 6.4.4 this is good news for terrorists, at home and abroad, as well as a useful source of income.[36]

Lord Colville repeated his musings about where the money wound up in his *Report on the Operation in 1991 of the Northern Ireland (Emergency Provisions) Act of 1991*. There he stated, with no disclosed basis, that "[c]onsidering the allegiance of some of those who thus exploit the system it is not fanciful to suppose that terrorist organizations take at least part of the damages awarded, so that they are being financed

[36]Viscount Colville of Culross QC, *Report on the Operation in 1991 of the Prevention of Terrorism (Temporary Provisions) Act of 1989*, at 19 (1992).

directly at the tax-payers expense."[37] Thus, he identified the claimants, *most* of whom had not been charged with an offense, with terrorist organizations, and implicitly identified their solicitors with the same organizations. This was worse than guilt by association, it was guilt by innuendo and smear.

Lord Colville met with members of the Lawyers Committee delegation and stressed that the aim of his comments was to criticize the authorities for settling claims too easily. He admitted, however, that there is no evidence that settlement money has gone into terrorist coffers. Rather, he declared, his conjecture is merely based on "common sense." Lord Colville also stated that he was not concerned that such speculation may put solicitors who seek compensation at greater risk, stating that anyone who represents IRA suspects is at risk to begin with; that risk is risk; and that no additional risk therefore accrues.[38]

Background Sources. Officials may imperil lawyers through slander intended to be circulated. Two instances involve recent books on the security situation that almost certainly rest on sources from within the RUC and the British Army.

In *Big Boys' Rules: The Secret Struggle Against the IRA*, Mark Urban wrote:

> There is undoubtedly a community of republican lawyers, supported financially by the movement, which is prepared to act in ways which might be considered unusual in Britain. For example, the lawyer may agree to pass a message from a terrorist to his commander, or might use cross-examination of a security forces witness

---

[37]Viscount Colville of Culross QC, *Report on the Operation in 1991 of the Northern Ireland (Emergency Provisions) Act 1991*, at 27 (1992).

[38]Lawyers Committee interview of Lord Colville, Sept. 2, 1992.

> in an attempt to prove whether an operation resulted in a leak within the IRA.[39]

Peter Madden, of Madden & Finucane, and Jane Winter, of British Irish Rights Watch, wrote to Urban taking issue with his remarks. Madden, while praising other aspects of the work, also cautioned Urban about relying too heavily on information from members of the security forces. Urban replied that "[t]he passage on page 74 does not convey my views on this subject effectively. Your letter and other representations have convinced me that it should not stand. I am resolved to change it as soon as the process of a new edition allows." He also acknowledged that Madden was correct in saying that, "my book is more like intelligence than evidence. There are obviously limitations in the way it was put together and I am open to constructive criticism."[40]

Martin Dillon made comparable assertions about defense lawyers and police sources in a book entitled *The Dirty War*. There he stated that:

> The only person allowed access to an arrested suspect is the suspect's solicitor. Solicitors who are "in the pay" of a terrorist organization can ask their clients what they have told their interrogators and can pass messages from an organization's leadership to their clients. In other words, solicitors can establish whether clients have compromised their terrorist overlords and accomplices or whether they are in a weak mental state and likely to break under continued questioning. . . . I spoke to police interrogators, who assured me that I was not dealing

---

[39]Mark Urban, *Big Boys' Rules: The Secret Struggle Against the IRA*, at 74 (1992).

[40]Letter dated June 19, 1992 from Mark Urban to Peter Madden. Urban also stated that, "I think that there are serious allegations against certain lawyers who represented republicans. I have never believed that these claims relate to any more than a small number of individuals. As for their veracity, I would prefer to save any detailed discussion for a face to face meeting." *See also Intimidation of Defence Lawyers Update, supra* note 35, at 1; Annex A.

> with the case of one rogue solicitor [who Dillon said elsewhere was not Patrick Finucane]. . . . Those extracts are a damning comment on one solicitor and they illustrate how terrorists can exploit the right of a solicitor to talk to a suspect while they are under interrogation. As I stated earlier, this is not an isolated case and it represents a much deeper malady. It happens away from public view, and this is the first time it has been documented.[41]

Replying to the President of the Law Society of Northern Ireland, the Chief Constable of the RUC, wrote: "I can state that the author, Martin Dillon, did not receive any police briefing whatsoever, upon which to found his allegations, nor was he supplied with any official documentation or statement of police views. In the absence of additional evidence no further police action is anticipated in this instance."[42] The Chief Constable carefully refrained from addressing the possibility, unequivocally alleged by Dillon, that police sources had supplied him with information unofficially. Considering the Chief Constable's careful circumlocution, there is no reason to discredit Dillon's allegation that police sources made the charge.

E. Complaints

Lawyers rarely lodge official complaints about police intimidation. Solicitors expressed a lack of faith in complaints procedures, frustration with the processing of complaints that were lodged, or both. This lack of faith applied in varying degrees to each official channel for pursuing grievances, whether the RUC, the Independent Commission for Police Complaints (ICPC), or the Law Society of Northern Ireland, the professional organization of solicitors. With regard to the official procedures, the solicitors' perception attests to the failure of the government to provide adequate safeguards, "[w]here

---

[41]Martin Dillon, *The Dirty War*, at 462-65 (1992).

[42]Quoted in British Irish Rights Watch, *Intimidation of Defence Lawyers*, *supra* note 35, at 8.

the security of lawyers is threatened as a result of discharging their functions."[43]

The reluctance of lawyers to file complaints about police misconduct does not stem from a fear to speak out publicly, though such a decision does carry obvious risks. Solicitors have been trying to publicize the problem of intimidation at least as early as 1987. In April of that year, an *ad hoc* committee of solicitors issued a brief public statement condemning threats made against defense lawyers by interrogators in detention centers and calling on the police to address the problem. Patrick Fahy, out of whose office the statement issued, recalled that an unusually large volume of threats and comments had prompted some action. About a dozen solicitors signed the statement, including Patrick Finucane. The statement received extensive coverage in the media. The RUC never responded.[44]

RUC. In a normal state, in which the police are held accountable, allegations of threats and other abuse by their members should be brought to the police. Peter Madden, among others, explained that solicitors have several reasons for not doing so in Northern Ireland. For one, complaining to the police about persistent intimidation by the police raises the unavoidable problem of the RUC's lack of accountability under present U.K. law.[45] For another, religion complicates matters insofar as the RUC is over 90% Protestant.[46] Patrick Duffy, the President of the Law Society, also noted that the police do not credit anything that most detainees say because as far as they are concerned the detainees are either terrorists or terrorist

---

[43]UN Basic Principles on the Role of Lawyers, No. 18.

[44]Lawyers Committee interview of Patrick Fahy, Sept. 1, 1992.

[45]For a discussion of the powers and accountability of the police, *see infra* pages 39-40, 85-87.

[46]Lawyers Committee interview of Geraldine Finucane and Peter Madden, Aug. 30, 1992.

sympathizers.[47] Finally, the track record of the RUC in handling such complaints has been miserable.

Several solicitors told us of lodging complaints with the RUC against their better judgment, only to have their judgment vindicated. Barra McGrory, for example, did go to the RUC's complaints branch concerning Conor McGuire and Martin O'Prey, his two clients who were later murdered. He did the same with regard to John McFadden and Henry Fitzsimmons, two other clients who reported mistreatment in Castlereagh. The only response McGrory has received from the RUC as a result of these complaints concerned McGuire, when two RUC officers gave the solicitor a leaflet on personal security and assured him they were looking into the matter.[48] Other solicitors likewise maintained that complaints they had filed had gone nowhere.

ICPC. A similar lack of confidence applies to the ICPC. In theory, the Commission supplies an independent civilian check on the complaints process by supervising RUC investigations of alleged police misconduct. In practice, solicitors maintain, this check is sadly inadequate. Practitioners report that they do not raise instances of intimidation with the ICPC in the first instance in part because the Commission must forward all complaints to the RUC in any event. Nor does ICPC involvement in the police inquiries that result allay traditional wariness about the RUC investigating itself. To the contrary, the most striking outcome of an RUC/ICPC investigation that the Lawyers Committee mission encountered from a lawyer's standpoint was the death threat, previously noted, made against a solicitor for having lodged a complaint in the first place.

Law Society. Few solicitors who agreed to speak to us expressed significant faith in their own association, the Law Society of Northern Ireland. The task of pursuing complaints about intimidation generally falls to the Society's president, who pursues matters mostly through private correspondence. The authorities respond with an acknowledgement of the president's concerns and little else.

---

[47]Lawyers Committee interview of Patrick Duffy, Aug. 26, 1992.

[48]Lawyers Committee interview of Barra McGrory, Sept. 1, 1992.

Committees, specifically the Human Rights Committee and the Criminal Law Committee, could provide a more effective and public mechanism but instead appear to have long been dormant. In part, this has to do with a feeling of frustration resulting from the unresponsiveness of police and government officials. In part, it reflects the additional risk that attaches to any solicitor pursuing controversial public matters against the security forces. Most of all, it underscores the startling lack of concern accorded the small minority of defense solicitors by their colleagues in civil practice. We are left with the impression that, for a large part of the legal profession in Northern Ireland, the obligation of lawyers to assert fundamental human rights against abuses by the state is a low priority; and if not the legal profession, who will do so?

II. THE MURDER OF PATRICK FINUCANE

The worst alleged instance of harassment of lawyers in Northern Ireland remains the killing of Patrick Finucane. The Lawyers Committee delegation found that Finucane had built an impressive practice in both criminal defense work and in challenging human rights abuses through litigation. We also found credible evidence that his very achievements subjected Finucane to the type of harassment that we have recounted defense solicitors in Northern Ireland still are said to face. Further, the Lawyers Committee mission found credible evidence suggesting collusion between elements within the security forces and loyalist paramilitaries in the Finucane murder. It is also clear, we conclude, that official responses have thus far been inadequate. In light of these conclusions, we again join Claire Palley, the U.K. government's nominee to the UN Sub-Commission on the Prevention of Discrimination and the Protection of Minorities, in calling on the U.K. government to establish "an independent public inquiry into the death of Mr. Finucane."

A. Finucane's Practice and Associations

How Patrick Finucane discharged his professional duties further illustrates the nature of defense and human rights practice in Northern Ireland; in particular, it shows that defense lawyers place themselves at risk and that innovative defense lawyers place themselves in peril.

Law Practice. Finucane established his practice in the 1970s and rose to prominence in the 1980s. A graduate of Trinity College Dublin, he eventually joined Peter Madden to form Madden & Finucane as a public interest law firm in 1979. Finucane soon became known for his work representing persons arrested under emergency legislation and their families. Finucane thus became part of a small community of practitioners, more fully described in Part I, whose work by definition meant repeated confrontation with the police. Perhaps more important, Finucane became well-known as a member of an even smaller set of solicitors who pioneered various legal devices for holding the authorities accountable for their actions.

Finucane's defense practice flourished throughout his career. Madden & Finucane eventually became a leader in defending individuals charged or detained under the emergency legislation. In part because Finucane was a Catholic who grew up in Belfast's heavily nationalist Falls Road area, his criminal law clientele frequently consisted of those accused of involvement with the IRA and other republican groups. Finucane's civil work involved both Catholic and Protestant clients, and there has never been a suggestion that he used religion or politics as a basis for representation. To the contrary, Mrs. Finucane stated after her husband's murder that, "Pat would have represented the people who shot him."[49]

Finucane also resorted to litigation to change the legal framework in which the security forces operated. This work, along with several high-profile criminal defense cases, made him a significantly greater thorn in the side of the authorities. These aspects of Finucane's practice also illustrate major human rights concerns in Northern Ireland in general and those that affect lawyers in particular.

- Hunger Strikes (1981) - Finucane first attained major prominence in connection with the much publicized hunger strikes in the Maze Prison in which persons convicted of paramilitary activity demanded political prisoner status. Among Finucane's activities was representing Bobby Sands, the first prisoner to die in the hunger strikes.[50]

- Compensation Claims - One of Finucane's most significant achievements was to help establish civil claims against the RUC as a permanent feature on the legal landscape. Such claims are common law tort actions for assault and false imprisonment. Most such claims are settled out of court on condition that the settlement remains secret. Nonetheless, detainees do receive some compensation, which commonly runs from several hundred to several thousand pounds.[51]

---

[49]Lawyers Committee interview of Geraldine Finucane and Peter Madden, Aug. 30, 1992.

[50]*Irish Times*, Feb. 13, 1989, at 11. For a brief history and recent survey of prison conditions in Northern Ireland, *see* Helsinki Watch, *Prison Conditions in the United Kingdom*, at 31-47 (June 1992).

[51]*See* Haldane Society, *Upholding the Rule of Law?*, at 24-25 (1992).

• Craigavon Shoot-To-Kill Inquest (1986) - Finucane won a major though short-lived precedent in representing the family of an individual shot dead allegedly under a "shoot-to-kill" policy maintained by the RUC. During the Coroner's inquiry into the death, known as the "Craigavon Inquest," Finucane left the proceedings on their first day to seek judicial review of a ruling that the officers involved in the incident could submit affidavits rather than testify subject to questioning. This case ultimately went to the Northern Ireland Court of Appeal, which ruled that the police could be called to give testimony.[52]

• Habeas Corpus (1988) - Finucane achieved another important result in *In Re Gillen's Application*, a case involving judicial review of a detention. While detained under the PTA, Brian Gillen was subjected to beatings and other physical mistreatment, for which he eventually received compensation. Finucane lodged the first successful habeas corpus action in which a detention was held to be unlawful when the police mistreated the detainee.[53]

• Casement Park Trials (1988) - One of Finucane's last major successes in criminal defense involved the case of Patrick McGeown. McGeown was among 41 individuals charged with offenses arising out of the highly publicized murder of two plainclothes British soldiers. The soldiers had driven into the funeral cortege of Caoimhin Mac Bradaigh (Kevin Brady), who had been killed in a loyalist attack on a funeral in the same nationalist neighborhood three days earlier. In November 1988, all charges against McGeown, including murder, were dropped at the preliminary inquiry into his case in the magistrate's court.[54]

• Media Ban (1988) - Finucane also represented Mitchell McLaughlin, a Sinn Fein representative elected to the Derry City Council, in a challenge to the British Home Secretary's 1988 media ban

---

[52]The House of Lords reversed the Court of Appeal and upheld the original rule in *McKerr* v. *Armagh Coroner*, [1990] 1 WLR 649, [1990] 1 All ER 865.

[53]*In re Gillen's Application*, (1988) NIJB 44 (QBD).

[54]Committee on the Administration of Justice, *The Casement Trials: A Case Study on the Right to a Fair Trial in Northern Ireland*, at 7 (1992).

on the broadcast of interviews of people representing Sinn Fein, a lawful political party identified with IRA positions. This ban, promulgated under the Broadcasting Act of 1981, was subsequently upheld in *R.* v. *Secretary of State for the Home Department ex parte Brind* (1991).[55]

- Prisoner Rights (1989) - The month before his death Finucane successfully challenged the way in which republican and loyalist prisoners who were held in solitary confinement were unlawfully denied a range of privileges for the purpose of punishment, including reading materials and adequate bedding.

- Derogation (1989) - On January 30, 1989, less than two weeks before his death, Finucane lodged two final applications with the European Commission on Human Rights under the European Convention on Human Rights, challenging the legality of the United Kingdom's derogation from the Convention in light of the European Court of Human Rights ruling that prolonged detention under the PTA was illegal. These cases, *Brannigan v. United Kingdom* and *McBride v. United Kingdom*, have yet to be finally adjudicated in the European Court of Human Rights.[56]

- Republican Associations - The authorities had another reason for disliking Finucane over which he had no control; namely, the alleged involvement of three of his brothers in the republican movement. One brother, John, whom the RUC alleged to have been an IRA member, was killed in an automobile accident in 1972. Another, Dermott, was convicted of IRA activities, escaped from the Maze Prison in 1983, and currently lives in the Irish Republic where he successfully fought extradition. The third brother, Seamus, was convicted of possession of guns and explosives in 1976 and released 10 years later. Since then he has been repeatedly detained without charge. Finucane represented both Dermott and Seamus, as the Madden & Finucane firm continues to do.

---

[55][1991] AC 696, [1991] 2 WLR 588, [1991] All ER 720.

[56]*Brannigan v. United Kingdom*, Application No. 14553/89; *McBride v. United Kingdom*, Application No. 14554/89.

The Lawyers Committee mission inquired about but found no evidence that Patrick Finucane was involved either in the republican activities of his brothers or in paramilitary activity generally. Apart from the UFF's allegations that he was a "PIRA officer," what suggestions of Finucane's IRA activity there have been have consisted either of unsupported newspaper references describing him as an "IRA solicitor," or allegations of derogatory statements about him made by the police during interrogation of his clients.

No one we interviewed on or off the record suggested that Finucane was in any way part of the IRA, no specific allegations of IRA activity against him have ever surfaced, and no complaint to that effect has ever been brought in any court or before the Northern Ireland Law Society. Two days after Finucane was killed, *The Guardian* reported that even "extreme loyalists were already slightly shamefaced about the murder, acknowledging that the lawyer had not been, as they claim publicly, a member of the IRA."[57] As noted, the Detective Superintendent in charge of the investigation into Finucane's killing specifically denied that Finucane was a member of the IRA. Instead, the officer added, Finucane was "regarded in police circles as very professional and discharged his duties with vigor and professionalism."

B. Prior Threats and Abuse

Not all authorities appear to have viewed Finucane with such high regard. There is substantial credible evidence suggesting that for several years prior to his killing he was a consistent target of official hostility and abuse. That evidence suggests that the abuse took at least three forms. First, police interrogators allegedly denigrated Finucane to his clients held in detention centers, particularly the Castlereagh detention center in Belfast. Second, this same group of interrogators apparently came to add threats, including death threats, to their alleged derogatory comments. Finally and especially distressing, a high government official issued what was in effect a thinly-veiled attack on certain Northern Ireland solicitors three weeks before Finucane was killed.

---

[57] *Guardian*, Feb. 14, 1989.

Abuse and Intimidation. Both Mrs. Finucane and Peter Madden indicated that the police had made derogatory comments about Finucane to his clients for years.[58] Several former clients, as well as Finucane's own recorded instructions from clients taken during meetings with them at detention centers, support these assertions. According to these sources, typical remarks included:

- Finucane would "do him no good."

- "I see you've asked for the Provie solicitor."

- "You must be a provie bastard because you got one as a solicitor."

- Finucane is "a fucking scum bastard."

- Finucane did not care about his clients but instead "went about in £250 suits."

- "He asked me who did I think I was sitting down and that I had obviously been talking to that 'dickhead' Finucane."

- Finucane was "an IRA man in a suit; another Provie on the payroll."[59]

Mrs. Finucane stated that until about a year before his death, her husband viewed such comments more as interrogation devices aimed at getting his clients to talk rather than as abuse directed at himself. The derisive commentary was so common that unless it was especially

---

[58]Lawyers Committee interview of Peter Madden, Aug. 24, 1992; and interview of Geraldine Finucane and Peter Madden, Aug. 30, 1992.

[59]Lawyers Committee interviews of Brian Austin, Seamus Finucane, Paul Finnegan, Patrick McDade, Aug. 31, 1992; Patrick Finucane, "Instructions Given by Brian Austin, Jan. 1989," at 1. (The Lawyers Committee obtained the permission of the client before citing any instructions to counsel.)

egregious, the instructions Finucane took would often simply note, "ref. to solic."[60]

Another picture of official attitudes toward Finucane comes from John Stalker, the former Deputy Chief Constable of Manchester who led an independent inquiry into the alleged "shoot to kill" deaths of six men at the hands of the RUC. His book about the inquiry, *Stalker*, reports on an encounter he had around 1984 or 1985 after talking with Finucane:

> . . . I recall one conversation with a youngish RUC uniformed sergeant who left his group and approached me angrily as I walked away after a very short conversation with a solicitor representing Martin McCauley, the youth who survived the shooting at the Hayshed. The sergeant came up to me and said, "May I speak with you Mr Stalker? Do you know who that was you were speaking to?" I replied, "Yes -- it was Martin McCauley and his solicitor." The sergeant said, "The solicitor is an IRA man -- any man who represents the IRA is an IRA man. His brother is an IRA man also and I have to say that I believe that a senior policeman of your rank should not be seen speaking to the likes of either of them. My colleagues have asked me to tell you that you have embarrassed all of us in doing that. I will be reporting this conversation and what you have done to my superiors."
>
> I was surprised at his studied vehemence, although I recognized his comment for the honest bigotry that it clearly was, and I let the matter go. But what he had starkly illustrated to me was the bitter depths of hatred even among professionals. . . . This conversation with the sergeant also showed me how easy it would be in the Province to have one's name included in Special Branch files and minds as having "possible Republican

---

[60]Lawyers Committee interview of Geraldine Finucane and Peter Madden, Aug. 30, 1992. *See, e.g.*, Patrick Finucane, "Instructions Given by Terrance O'Neill, Sept. 19, 1988."

sympathies." An open conversation with a solicitor who performs his duty to the courts was, it seems, probably sufficient evidence of such "sympathies."[61]

Death Threats. Several sources told us that threats had also long been a feature of the abuse directed at Finucane. One client, for example, stated that as early as 1984 interrogators told him that Finucane "would be like you; he'd be fuckin' blown away." According to Peter Madden, the problem of occasional threats went back to the late 1970s.[62]

There is credible evidence that the threats became more serious and persistent in the year prior to Finucane's murder. Mrs. Finucane traced the escalation to her husband's involvement with the Brian Gillen case in January 1988. She based her recollection both on direct threats phoned to the Finucane home and on remarks her husband made about what his clients had been telling him.[63]

Statements by former clients, together with instructions from clients that Finucane recorded at the time, support Mrs. Finucane's impression. One is Gillen himself, who asserted that after Finucane had filed the habeas petition on his behalf, his interrogators began to attack the solicitor, making such comments as, "It would be better if he were dead than defending the likes of you," and "we can give them [detained loyalists paramilitary members] his details along with yours." Another client detained that year stated that his interrogators echoed these

---

[61]John Stalker, *Stalker*, at 49 (1988).

[62]Lawyers Committee interview of Patrick McDade, Aug. 31, 1992; and interview of Peter Madden, Aug. 24, 1992.

[63]Mrs. Finucane attempted to present evidence concerning these death threats at the Coroner's Inquest, but was denied the opportunity to be heard. Lawyers Committee interview with Geraldine Finucane and Peter Madden, Aug. 30, 1992. In a letter to British Irish Rights Watch dated May 8, 1992, Martin Finucane also alleged that his brother received telephoned death threats before he died. British Irish Rights Watch, *The Murder of Patrick Finucane: Report to the Lawyers Committee for Human Rights*, at 3 (1992). *See also* Amnesty International, *United Kingdom: Human Rights Concerns*, at 56 (June 1991).

sentiments, saying, "we'll give Pat Finucane the same as Mairaid Farrell [who was killed in the Gibraltar shootings] got," adding, "we'll just drop your name and Pat's name to the UDA."

In early 1989 the threats became urgent. One client, detained on January 5, said that the police told him, "Finucane is an IRA man. He's a dead man. He'll be dead within three months." This client also told us that the interrogators also asked details about Finucane as well as whether it was Finucane or Peter Madden who was really running the firm." One further statement was a message for Finucane: "The message was that, 'You judge a person's character by his company and Mr. Finucane's company was made up of murderers, blackmailers, gangsters, etc.' He [the detective] told me to tell him, that he is a 'Thug in a suit,' a person trying to let on he is doing a job and that like every other Fenian bastard he would meet his end." Still another client, detained two days later, told us the remarks to him were even more dire. According to this individual, the interrogators said that, "Fucking Finucane's getting took out," and to "tell his fucking brother [Seamus Finucane] that he's nothing but scum and that he's going to be taken out too."[64]

Official Statements. At about this time in London official statements were being made which served to increase the risk for solicitors in Finucane's position.

The statements came from Douglas Hogg MP, then Parliamentary Under-Secretary of State for the Home Office. On January 17, 1989, Hogg addressed certain new provisions during a committee debate on the Prevention of Terrorism (Temporary Provisions) Bill. One provision would have prohibited any disclosure likely to prejudice an investigation into paramilitary activity. The other would have criminalized any failure by a person to disclose information that he or she knew or believed might assist in preventing an act of terrorism or in securing the apprehension, prosecution or conviction of a person for a scheduled offense. Members had proposed amendments aimed at

---

[64]Lawyers Committee interviews of Seamus Finucane, Brian Austin, and Patrick McDade, Aug. 31, 1992; and interview of Brian Gillen, Sept. 1, 1992; Patrick Finucane, "Instructions Given by Brian Austin, Jan. 1989,"; Patrick Finucane, "Instructions Given by Patrick McDade, Jan. 7, 1989."

preserving attorney/client confidentially against the encroachments that these new provisions threatened. In defending those encroachments, Mr. Hogg stated:

> I have to state as a fact, but with great regret, that there are in Northern Ireland a number of solicitors who are unduly sympathetic to the cause of the IRA. -- [Interruption.] I repeat that there are in the Province a number of solicitors who are unduly sympathetic to the cause of the IRA. One has to bear that in mind.[65]

Seamus Mallon, Social Democratic Labour Party Member for Newry and Armagh, immediately challenged Hogg, stating:

> That is a remarkable statement for a Minister to make about members of a profession who have borne much of the heat in a traumatic and abnormal situation. Such words should not be said without the courage to support them. I find it appalling that the Minister should make such an accusation with such emphasis and without, it seems, the intention of substantiating it."[66]

Rather than substantiate his allegations, Hogg merely repeated them, saying: "I state it on the basis of advice that I have received, guidance that I have been given by people who are dealing with these matters, and I shall not expand on it further."[67]

Later in the debate Mallon prophetically observed:

> I have no doubt that there are lawyers walking the streets or driving on the roads of the North of Ireland who have become targets for assassins' bullets as a result of the statement that has been made tonight. . . . Following the

---

[65]*Hansard*, House of Commons, Standing Committee B., Jan. 17, 1989, at col. 508.

[66]*Id.*, at col. 509.

[67]*Id.*, at col. 511.

> Minister's statement, people's lives are in grave danger. People who have brought cases to the European Court against this legislation will be suspected. People accused of IRA membership and other activities will be suspected. We have thrown a blanket over many lawyers in the North of Ireland, and it will be on the head of this Minister and Government if the assassin's bullet decides to do, by lead, what this Minister has done, by word.[68]

Hogg's remarks caused a public outcry, especially from within Northern Ireland's legal community. Mrs. Finucane told us that her husband was especially shocked. Not only could he not understand why a government minister would make so irresponsible a statement, he also began to take the threats against him as more than interrogation devices. After Finucane's murder, another outcry against Hogg arose that included calls for his resignation, but these went unheeded. Hogg has since moved on to another post. To date, neither he nor the government has issued an apology for his remarks save for feeble expressions of regret at Finucane's killing. Hogg also refused to meet with our delegation to discuss his remarks.

C. Evidence Suggesting Collusion

Anyone looking into Patrick Finucane's assassination quickly encounters a staggering array of stories, incidents, and theories pointing to official involvement in the crime. Many of these would be incredible were not other instances of complicity already established. The Lawyers Committee delegation did not realistically expect to prove or disprove allegations of collusion, much less to "solve" the murder itself. If the information we gathered demonstrates anything, it is that only a fresh, independent inquiry armed with such powers as the authority to administer oaths and issue subpoenas could have any hope of achieving these goals. What follows is the evidence that leads to this conclusion.

---

[68] *Id.*, at col. 519.

The Army Connection. Substantial evidence suggests the complicity of the British Army. This link emerged as a result of the trial of Brian Nelson.

Nelson was a double agent recruited by British military intelligence who for two years served as the chief intelligence officer of the UDA. Nelson's UDA post meant that the responsibility for targeting victims of loyalist death squads fell to him. Theoretically, Nelson was supposed to supply his Army handlers with information about loyalist operations, especially planned killings. The Army was then to share its information with the RUC. Yet things did not always work out this way. Several murders that Nelson helped plan in fact took place. It remains unclear to this day whether this occurred because Nelson "got out of hand," because the Army hoarded its information out of a sense of rivalry with the RUC, or because of some other reason. Nelson was eventually arrested in January 1990 and charged with murder and lesser offenses. The murder charges were later dropped "in the interest of justice," and Nelson was convicted on five counts of conspiracy to murder and was sentenced to 10 years imprisonment.

The most prominent UDA victim during Nelson's time was Patrick Finucane. Suspicions of Nelson's involvement in that murder arose as early as the Coroner's Inquest in September 1990. The extent of this involvement did not begin to become clear, however, until Nelson agreed to speak about his activities to the producers of a BBC *Panorama* documentary broadcast on June 8, 1992. The program also relied on a journal Nelson had kept that had come into the possession of the documentary's writers, John Ware and Geoffrey Seed.

The material developed by *Panorama* and other sources indicates that the Army knew that Finucane was in danger as early as December, 1988. Nelson had written in this journal that "[s]ome two months before the actual shooting I was asked by 'R' [later identified as a leading UDA assassin] to see what I could dig up on Finucane. At the time I informed my handlers that 'R' was showing interest in the solicitor." The journal adds that Nelson passed the photograph of Finucane to R on the Thursday before the killing. It also states that Nelson told his handlers that the UDA was interested in targeting not only Finucane but P.J. McGrory as well.[69]

According to one source, the initial incident Nelson described took place when the local newspapers printed a photograph of Finucane and Patrick McGeown leaving the Crumlin Road Courthouse after charges against McGeown had been dismissed in the Casement Trials. R asked Nelson for information about "the man in the photo." When Nelson responded with information about McGeown, R then asked for material about Finucane as well. Prior to the release of the journal entry, Nelson's principal Army handler, a man known only as "Colonel J," testified at Nelson's trial that the Army only knew about the targeting of McGeown.[70] Those portions of Nelson's journal made public thus far do not support this assertion. Official sources we interviewed would take no position on the timing of these events, but did assure us that Nelson's involvement in the Finucane killing could be inferred.

The RUC Connection. There is also evidence pointing to the involvement of the RUC. RUC complicity may not only have taken the form of knowing acquiescence but of actual instigation.

Patrick McGeown, the other "man in the photo," told the Lawyers Committee mission that he was stopped by a joint RUC/Army patrol two or three days after Finucane had secured his release from the Crumlin Road Jail. An RUC officer called him aside and said, "[d]on't think you got away with that. We intend to make sure you won't be about too long." What made the incident unusual, McGeown thought, was that the officer added, "[a]nd your mate Pat, we'll fix him too." McGeown did not pay much attention to the threat until early in December 1988, when a loyalist group produced a magazine with articles threatening both McGeown and Finucane with murder. The magazine also had a photograph of him with a beard that was taken while he was in prison. McGeown stated that the only time he was other than clean

---

[69] Script of *Panorama*, dated June 6, 1992 (for BBC broadcast of June 8, 1992); *Independent*, June 9, 1992, at 3.

[70] Testimony of Colonel "J", *R.* v. *Nelson*, High Court of Justice, trial transcript at 16-17 (1992).

shaven was when he was in prison, and that the photograph therefore had to originate from an official source.[71]

Two independent sources told us that the RUC also had a double agent in the UDA. They stated that they had learned from loyalist sources that in late December 1988 or early January 1989 Brian Nelson came to a UFF meeting and passed a file on Finucane to R. Those present took the transfer of this file to mean than Finucane would be killed. A week later the double agent alerted his handlers in the RUC Special Branch who were stationed at Castlereagh. About two weeks later, R came to the agent and asked him for weapons, including a Browning. At his next meeting with his handlers, the agent told them of R's request and that he would be supplying the weapons in the next few days. In both instances, the agent gave the information to his handlers on the assumption that they would do something to prevent the murder from taking place.

About this time, approximately three weeks before the murder, some police officers may have taken on an active role. One source our delegation considered reliable, who maintained loyalist contacts, told us that two or three mid-level RUC officers intruded upon the normal questioning of three UDA men detained at Castlereagh. The UDA detainees were members of a squad of about a dozen assassins known as "the military men." Specifically, the detainees were members of the West Belfast military men, the area in which Brian Nelson operated and which had overlapping jurisdiction over the neighborhood where Finucane lived.

The officers allegedly asked the detectives interrogating the detainees, "did you tell them about the treble?" By "treble" they meant Finucane, P.J. McGrory, in the opinion of many the dean of Northern Ireland defense solicitors, and Oliver Kelly, another prominent defense solicitor. At this point, both the officers and the detectives told the UDA men to forget about indiscriminate sectarian killings and concentrate on these three solicitors as the "brains behind the IRA." One journalist stressed that this account was based on extremely reliable authority. He also noted that this was the most institutionalized instance of targeting

---

[71]Lawyers Committee interview of Patrick McGeown, Sept. 3, 1992.

that he had encountered. Asked why the hit squad was not contacted on the outside, another journalist replied that it was simply easier to pass information in Castlereagh because the military men were often detained and because there were no records of what went on.

According to another source, the Special Branch had one last opportunity to prevent the killing just hours before it occurred. On the day Finucane was murdered, an adjutant UFF commander under R called the RUC's agent at about 3:00 p.m. This adjutant told R to deliver the weapons to a nearby social club at 5:00 p.m., which he did. He then called his Special Branch handlers; told them that he had handed over the guns; and impressed upon them that he thought they would be used quickly. By 7:30 p.m., Finucane was dead.

The Committee. A somewhat different account of official involvement came to light in a television documentary entitled, "The Committee," which was broadcast on October 2, 1991 as part of Channel 4's *Dispatches* series.

The program alleged the existence of a central coordinating committee, with up to 60 members, drawn from the UDA, UFF, UVF, the Protestant Action Force, the RUC, and prominent loyalist businessmen, professionals, and politicians. The ostensible purpose of this group is to sanction the assassination of purported republicans and coordinate the operations of RUC extremists and loyalist paramilitary operatives in carrying out killings as planned. Such coordination can occur, the documentary contended, due to a group of committed loyalists within the RUC who have organized themselves into a group known as the "Inner Force" or "Inner Circle." This Inner Force allegedly participates in the Central Coordinating Committee.[72]

The *Dispatches* program asserted that the Committee organized the murder of Patrick Finucane. Ben Hamilton, the main researcher for Box Productions, the independent company that produced the program, expanded on this assertion in conversations with British Irish Rights

[72]Script of "The Committee" for *Dispatches*, dated Oct. 2, 1991, at 6-10 (for Channel 4 television broadcast of same date).

Watch and with our delegation.[73] Hamilton contends that his principal source was present at the meeting of the Committee that targeted Finucane. According to this individual, known as "Source A," this meeting took place in an Orange Hall in Belfast two weeks before the killing. The source asserted that the idea for the killing came from Brian Nelson and was proposed to the Committee by members of the Inner Force. The Committee allegedly decided to go ahead with the murder for two reasons. First, it understood Douglas Hogg's comments to be a green light from the government. Second, Nelson had both Army and RUC intelligence files purporting to show that Finucane had met with IRA officials in Belfast and Dublin. The very quality of intelligence that Nelson could often provide led the Committee to suspect that he was a double agent. Consequently, the group decided to let him organize the murder on his own rather than commission a UFF assassination squad directly.

Hamilton, Box Productions, and Channel 4 have since been brought to court on charges of violating Section 19 of the PTA, which mandates the disclosure of information relating to paramilitary activity. Despite having turned over much of their information to the RUC, the defendants were fined £75,000 for contempt of court for not disclosing the identity of Source A. Hamilton was also arrested by Scotland Yard detectives acting for the RUC and held for questioning on the same grounds. He has since been released and the charges have been dropped.[74]

A number of journalists we interviewed expressed skepticism about the Committee's existence. As for the Inner Force or Circle, some

---

[73]Lawyers Committee interview of Ben Hamilton, Sept. 2, 1992; British Irish Rights Watch, *The Murder of Patrick Finucane: Report to the Lawyers Committee for Human Rights*, at Annex 5 (1992).

[74]*Guardian*, Nov. 24, 1992, at E40.

detainees have alleged that RUC detectives have made reference to such a group during interrogation.[75]

The Lawyers Committee is not in a position to confirm or deny any particular account of the crime. We do conclude that there is sufficient evidence of the security forces' prior knowledge of the murder plot to warrant an official inquiry by an agency with subpoena power independent of those forces.

D. Official Responses

No one has been tried, charged, or even arrested for Patrick Finucane's murder. One senior official told our mission that the killers are known and are currently serving time for other offenses. Even if true, this coincidence does not satisfy the public's need for justice, put to rest concern about official involvement in the crime, or excuse the authorities continuing failure to resolve the matter once and for all.

Police Investigation. The RUC refused to discuss any aspect of the Finucane case with us on the ground that the investigation was ongoing. If there has been an ongoing investigation, it has been singularly unproductive.

In testimony at the September 1990 Coroner's Inquest, Detective Superintendent Simpson stated that the RUC began operating on the assumption that the UFF committed the murder even before the organization claimed credit the next day. Simpson added that the police interrogated at least 14 UFF members about the killing and were "reasonably sure that the main perpetrators of the murder were among these suspects," but that "no evidence is presently available to sustain a charge of murder." He also pointed out that on July 4, 1989, the RUC arrested three young men in the Shankill Road area for UFF membership

[75]According to one detainee, the police were "talking about the Inner Circle. They mentioned the late Mr Finucane. They said they might as well get the road sweeps moving to get the scum off and the dirt out of the road." Madden & Finucane, Submission to the (UN) Committee Against Torture, app. at 27 (case 52) (Nov. 13, 1991).

and for possession of two guns, one of which was the 9mm pistol used in the assassination. Each of the three -- David Anderson, Frank Arbuthnot, and William Barr -- was convicted and sentenced to a young offenders center. None of the evidence indicated that any of these individuals took part in the killing itself. The NIO has stressed to us, however, that these convictions resulted from the murder investigation. It is not apparent why, given the RUC's extraordinary powers of interrogation, it has been unable to tie the weapon to an assassin.

A great deal of what would appear the most basic investigatory work remains undone. To date, the RUC has made no effort to interview Geraldine Finucane, Peter Madden, or any Madden & Finucane client concerning the threats made in Castlereagh or the statements made by Douglas Hogg. This failure is all the more striking given Mrs. Finucane's public statements at the time of the Coroner's Inquest, various press accounts, the Liberty report by the international delegation of lawyers and submissions to the United Nations by British Irish Rights Watch.

Stevens Inquiry. The RUC has publicly stated that it did not pursue the possibility of security forces collusion in the murder out of deference to the Stevens Inquiry. This referred to an investigation conducted by John Stevens, then Deputy Chief Constable of the Cambridgeshire Police, who was invited in 1989 by RUC Chief Constable Hugh Annesley to examine charges of collusion between members of the security forces and loyalist paramilitaries following the disappearance of police photo-montages and alleged leaks in the loyalist murder of Loughlin Maginn. Mr. Stevens concluded the inquiry on May 17, 1990, producing a classified report as well as issuing a public summary of his findings and recommendations.[76] Since then, Chief Constable Annesley has asked Mr. Stevens, who is now Chief Constable for the Northumbria Police, to investigate additional allegations made in the BBC's *Panorama* documentary regarding Brian Nelson.

---

[76]John Stevens, "Summary of the Report of the Deputy Chief Constable of Cambridgeshire into Allegations of Collusion between Members of the Security Forces and Loyalist Paramilitaries" (May 1990).

During the Coroner's Inquest, Detective Superintendent Simpson testified that any allegations of official collusion in the murder were turned over to the Stevens Inquiry, with which he "liaised closely." He added that, "[n]o evidence was found substantiating the allegation but rather substantial evidence to the contrary." One official source did not dispute this conclusion, but did tell the Lawyers Committee delegation that it was premature when it was made.

The Stevens Inquiry led to numerous reforms for keeping security information out of paramilitary hands. It also led to the prosecution of 59 members of the UDR and loyalist groups for various types of collusion, the vast majority from the latter category. Among this number is Brian Nelson. Despite these results, leaks of official information to paramilitary groups continue to be a problem in Northern Ireland.[77]

The Stevens Inquiry has not, however, resulted in prosecution for the Finucane murder. Nor were efforts made to contact Mrs. Finucane, Finucane's colleagues at his firm, or his former clients. Mr. Stevens, who met with members of our delegation, told us that limited time, resources, and terms of reference prevented his inquiry from tracking down every lead in the Finucane case. He added that anything that was uncovered would properly have been turned over to the RUC.[78] Sources have suggested to the Lawyers Committee mission that such evidence as was uncovered pointed to collusion between Nelson and the Army rather than with the RUC.

Coroner's Inquest. The Coroner's Inquest has so far yielded almost all of the official information about the Finucane killing that is available publicly. The Inquest was conducted by John Leckey, who met with a member of the Lawyers Committee delegation. The Inquest produced one controversy when Mrs. Finucane attempted to submit a

---

[77]While the Lawyers Committee delegation was in Northern Ireland, for example, a copy of an Army photograph montage of republican suspects was sent to a newspaper in Antrim. One of the men pictured in the montage had earlier been shot to death by the UDA. *Independent*, Sept. 3, 1992.

[78]Lawyers Committee interview of Chief Constable John Stevens, Sept. 4, 1992.

statement concerning the threats made to her husband in Castlereagh. When the RUC's counsel objected, Leckey ruled the statement inadmissible on the grounds of irrelevancy. Leckey did, however, permit the head of the investigation to be questioned about the death threats. Mrs. Finucane also released her statement to the press.

Law Society and Bar Council. Given the murder of a prominent colleague, the response by Northern Ireland's two main lawyers associations was tepid. This assessment is not meant to be a comment on individuals so much as an observation about the inhibitions preventing the Northern Ireland legal profession from acting in a concerted fashion.

The day after Finucane was shot, the President of the Law Society issued a statement condemning it. A public meeting of solicitors was held shortly thereafter, but no decision on official Law Society action resulted. Successive Law Society presidents have taken the Finucane matter up privately with the authorities, but have received no satisfaction. The organization also reinstituted its committee on human rights, but most solicitors we spoke with said this committee remains passive. As a group, the Law Society has yet to make any call for a public inquiry into the Finucane killing or to publicly criticize the authorities for lack of results.

The Bar Council, which represents barristers, did nothing.[79]

---

[79] *Irish Times*, Feb. 14, 1989, at 6; Lawyers Committee interviews of Patrick Duffy, then President of the Law Society of Northern Ireland, Aug. 26 & Sept. 3, 1992; and P.J. McGrory, Sept. 2 & 3, 1992.

III. LAWYERS AND THE LEGAL FRAMEWORK

The legal setting in Northern Ireland all but ordains that defense lawyers suffer intimidation. Together the EPA and PTA give the security forces every incentive to rely on custodial interrogation as their primary means of obtaining convictions. Practices and conditions within the detention centers facilitate this incentive. The overall approach the law establishes makes legal counsel more crucial and therefore more open to police hostility. Far from checking this hostility, the law encourages it, often in dangerous ways. Complaints procedures, which might provide a measure of redress, remain ineffectual, prompting the skepticism solicitors accord the complaints process and contributing to their tenuous position in the system itself.

A. The Seven Decade Emergency

Features of the Northern Ireland emergency laws that do not directly pertain to defense lawyers outright nonetheless affect them profoundly. The PTA and EPA cut down the traditional laws of England to get to the devil of terrorism. The extent to which they do so can be gleaned from a comparison with pre-emergency provisions, the PACE Order, and international agreements to which the U.K. is a party. The emergency laws and related case law attempt to extirpate political violence by allowing for prolonged detention, ready admissibility of confessions and, most recently, the diminution of the right to silence. The RUC takes full advantage of the emphasis on confessions, asserting that paramilitary activity makes forensic evidence and testimony from witnesses hard to come by. As Lord Colville points out, detainees therefore bear the brunt of this system.[80] In such an atmosphere solicitors are stumbling blocks.

Detention. Under the PTA, an individual may be held without charge for as long as seven days. Section 14 of the Act provides that a constable may arrest someone based upon reasonable suspicion of terrorist activity, and that that individual "shall not be detained on right of arrest for more than forty-eight hours after arrest." The statute adds, however, that:

---

[80]Lawyers Committee interview of Lord Colville, Sept. 2, 1992.

> The Secretary of State may, in a particular case, extend the period of forty-eight hours . . . but any such further period or periods shall not exceed five days in all and if an application for such an extension is made, the person detained shall as soon as practicable be given written notice of that fact and of the time when the application was made.[81]

These provisions stand in marked contrast to "ordinary" criminal standards. Under the PACE Order, detention without charge ordinarily cannot last longer than 24 hours. This period may be extended an additional 12 hours, but only if an officer of at least the rank of superintendent has reasonable grounds for believing that additional time is necessary to secure evidence in a case involving a serious arrestable offense. Detention beyond 36 hours can only be authorized by a magistrates' court, and then only in a maximum of 36-hour increments, and in no case beyond 96 hours.[82]

Extensions under the PTA regularly occur. In 1991, of 1,680 who were arrested under the PTA, extensions were granted in 495 instances: 14 for one additional day; 209 for two days; 229 for up to three days; 39 for up to four days; and five for five additional days.[83]

The protracted detentions that the PTA promotes have been successfully challenged as a violation of international human rights standards. In *Brogan v. United Kingdom*, the European Court of Human Rights held that a detention under the PTA which exceeded four days and six hours violated Article 5(3) of the European Convention on Human Rights. Rather than amend the PTA, the United Kingdom responded by derogating from the European Convention. The government justified this derogation on the ground that decisions to detain suspects "may be, and

---

[81]Prevention of Terrorism (Temporary Provisions) Act of 1989, § 14(1)-(5).

[82]Police and Criminal Evidence (Northern Ireland) Order of 1989, arts. 42(1), 43(1), 44 & 45.

[83]Viscount Colville of Culross QC, *Report on the Operation in 1991 of the Prevention of Terrorism (Temporary Provisions) Act 1989*, at Tables 6 & 7 (1992).

often are, taken on the basis of information, the nature and source of which could not be revealed to a suspect or his [or her] legal advisor without serious risk to individuals helping the police or the prospect of further valuable intelligence being lost."[84] It was this decision to derogate which Patrick Finucane challenged in the still pending actions of *Brannigan v. United Kingdom* and *McBride v. United Kingdom*.

Confessions. Just as some emergency provisions give the police the time needed to obtain confessions, others insure that confessions and other incriminating statements are readily admissible. Specifically, under Section 11 of the 1991 amendments to the EPA, a person on trial for a scheduled offense wishing to challenge the admissibility of a statement must adduce *prima facie* evidence not merely that the incriminating statement was involuntary, but that he or she:

> was subjected to torture, to inhuman or degrading treatment, or to any violence or threat of violence (whether or not amounting to torture) in order to induce him [or her] to make the statement.[85]

Once a such *prima facie* showing is made, the burden shifts to the prosecution to prove beyond a reasonable doubt that the alleged torture, inhuman or degrading treatment, violence, or threat of violence did not take place.

Section 5 further codifies the common law principle that judges have the discretion to exclude otherwise admissible confessions, "if it appears to the court that it is appropriate to do so in order to avoid unfairness to the accused or otherwise in the interests of justice."[86]

---

[84]David Waddington, then Home Secretary, quoted in Helsinki Watch Report, *supra* note 2, at note 28.

[85]Northern Ireland (Emergency Provisions) Act of 1987, § 5 (supplanting former § 8 of the 1978 EPA with § 8(2)(b)).

[86]Northern Ireland (Emergency Provisions) Act, § 5 (supplanting former § 8 of the 1978 EPA with § 8(3)).

These provisions represent a step forward, but only because the preceding standards were even more indulgent. The section which the 1987 amendments replaced allowed into evidence a statement obtained by the police unless the defendant produced *prima facie* evidence that he or she "was subjected to torture or to inhuman or degrading treatment in order to induce him to make the statement."[87] Under this standard, some courts admitted confessions even when there was evidence of physical abuse, to say nothing of threats and other psychological pressure.[88]

The current EPA standards compare unfavorably with the common law or the PACE Order. Under the common law, the admissibility of confessions turned on whether they were voluntary. Judicially drafted strictures, known as the Judges Rules, defined "voluntary" as "not obtained . . . by fear of prejudice or hope of advantage, exercised or held out by a person in authority, or by oppression."[89] The "voluntariness principle" controlled all prosecutions in Northern Ireland until the enactment of the EPA in 1973, and "ordinary" criminal cases until the PACE Order of 1989. PACE altered the traditional standard. Under Article 74, a prosecutor need only prove that a statement was not obtained by "oppression of the person who made it or in consequence of anything said or done that was likely to render it unreliable." The same article defines "oppression" as "including" the same impermissible actions described in the EPA. The term "include," however, clearly indicates that practices permissible under the EPA could result in exclusion of evidence under PACE.[90]

---

[87]Northern Ireland (Emergency Provisions) Act, 1973, § 8.

[88]*See R. v. McCormick*, (1977) N.I. 105 ("a moderate degree of physical maltreatment for the purpose of inducing a person to make a statement" permissible). *But see R. v. O'Halloran*, (1979) 2 NIJB (CA) ("physical violence" impermissible).

[89]Judges Rules, para. 3 (1964).

[90]Police and Criminal Evidence (Northern Ireland) Order of 1989, art. 74. *See* Committee on the Administration of Justice, *Civil Liberties in Northern Ireland*, at 42-43 (1990) [hereinafter CAJ, *Civil Liberties*].

The current standards of admissibility insure that confessions remain the "dominant reality of trials in the Diplock courts."[91] One independent study conducted in 1981 found that the Director of Public Prosecutions relied on confessions in 89% of all scheduled offense cases.[92] The report of a commission headed by Judge H.G. Bennett QC, issued three years earlier, estimated that confessions furnished the sole basis for conviction 75% to 80% of the time.[93] According to the Committee on the Administration of Justice, these percentages have not changed significantly since.[94] As one journalist told our delegation, the RUC generally looks to informers and confessions first, forensics second, and nothing third.

Substantial evidence also suggests that the current standards, which by definition allow involuntary confessions, also produce persistent mistreatment of detainees. In its recent report on Northern Ireland, Helsinki Watch recorded numerous specific allegations of abuse and brutality.[95] The Committee on the Administration of Justice, Amnesty International, British Irish Rights Watch, and the Haldane Society have done the same.[96] Investigating this mistreatment was beyond the terms of reference for this Lawyers Committee mission. That said, both detainees and solicitors made abundantly clear to us that whatever abuse the authorities directed at lawyers paled in comparison

---

[91]NYC Bar Report, *supra* note 2, at 68.

[92]Dermott Walsh, *The Use and Abuse of Emergency Legislation in Northern Ireland* (1983).

[93]Report of the Commission of Inquiry into Police Interrogation Procedures n Northern Ireland, at 10 (Mar. 19, 1979).

[94]Committee on the Administration of Justice, *A Briefing Paper on the Northern Ireland (Emergency Provisions) Bill*, at 15 (1990).

[95]Helsinki Watch Report, *supra* note 2, at 36-40, and app. A.

[96]Committee on the Administration of Justice, *Submission to the United Nations Committee Against Torture* (Nov. 13, 1991); Amnesty International, *United Kingdom: Allegations of Ill-Treatment in Northern Ireland* (Nov. 1991); *Intimidation of Defence Lawyers, supra* note 35; Haldane Society, *Criminal Justice Under the "Emergency Powers" in the 1990s*, at 13-20 (1992).

to what they assert those actually brought into the detention centers face, often on a regular basis.

Right to Silence. The regular use of questionable confessions makes the effective exercise of the right to silence paramount. Recent assaults on that right make such exercise more difficult and timely advice from counsel more crucial.

The current standard derives from the Criminal Evidence (Northern Ireland) Order of 1988. This order provides that a negative inference may be drawn from pre-trial silence in three situations and from silence during the trial in one circumstance. Article 3 permits such inferences when an accused bases his or her criminal defense on some fact which he or she failed to mention during police questioning but which the defendant could reasonably have been expected to raise. Article 5 permits adverse inferences when a defendant fails to give the police an explanation for the presence of an object, substance, or mark on or near his or her person that could reasonably be believed to result from the defendant's participation in a crime. Under Article 6, a defendant risks a negative inference when the accused fails to account for his or her whereabouts at the time a crime was committed. Under a Code of Practice issued pursuant to the PACE Order, the police are required to inform individuals of the adverse effects that refusal to answer questions might bring.[97] The rule is as if a failure to respond after receiving a *Miranda* warning from a police officer in the United States would be admissible evidence of guilt.[98] Finally, Article 4 permits the court or a jury to draw negative inferences from a defendant's refusal to answer questions at the trial.

As Peter Burns observed in his official comments before the (UN) Committee Against Torture, these provisions effectively eliminate

---

[97]CAJ, *Civil Liberties, supra* note 90, at 50-52, 55-56.

[98]In *Miranda*, the Supreme Court of the United States held that the prosecution may not use statements made by a defendant during custodial interrogation unless the law enforcement officers conducting the interrogation have given the defendant adequate warnings of his or her constitutional rights, including the right to remain silent. *Miranda* v. *Arizona*, 384 U.S. 436, 467-79 (1966).

the right to silence.[99] Specifically, they dilute standards previously in force and violate international human rights protections. Under the common law standard, neither the prosecution nor the trial judge could suggest to the jury that an adverse inference could be drawn from a defendant's silence when questioned by the police.[100] Article 14(3)(g) of the International Covenant on Civil and Political Rights, which the United Kingdom has signed, guarantees that "[i]n the determination of any criminal charge against him [or her], everyone shall be entitled to the following minimum guarantees . . . [including]. . . [n]ot to be compelled to testify against himself [or herself] or to confess guilt." Insofar as it permits adverse inferences from silence, the Criminal Evidence Order violates this Covenant.

After some initial hesitation, judges in Northern Ireland are drawing negative inferences from silence freely.[101] In *R. v. Smith*, Lord Justice Kelly first held that an inference under the Order should be drawn only where the evidence otherwise produced by the prosecution approached being beyond a reasonable doubt.[102] Just over a year later, in *R. v. McLernon*, the Lord Justice expanded the Order's application in a case involving a defendant charged with possession of a firearm who had remained silent for six days but gave a partial account on the seventh.[103] Here the court held that a refusal to answer questions may be considered when it merely adds weight to the prosecution's case. In

---

[99]Burns stated: "[I]n Northern Ireland, a different set of rules applied to the interrogation of persons suspected of terrorism and there was in effect no right of silence." Comments of Peter Burns, Country Rapporteur, (UN) Committee Against Torture, Seventh Session, Summary of the 91st Meeting, UN Doc. CAT/C/SR.91, at 5 (Nov. 13 1991) [hereinafter Burns Comments to CAT].

[100]The only exception to this rule related to instances in which two people were talking on even terms and one accused the other of some action in circumstances in which a denial would be expected but did not come. CAJ, *Civil Liberties, supra* note 90, at 51.

[101]*See generally* Haldane Society, *Northern Ireland: Criminal Justice Under the "Emergency Powers" in the 1990s*, at 42-47 (1992).

[102]*R. v. Smith*, Northern Ireland Court of Appeal, (transcript), Oct. 20, 1989.

[103]*R. v. McLernon*, Northern Ireland Court of Appeal, (transcript), April 1, 1992.

R. v. Morrison, Martin et al., the Court of Appeal held that the Order permitted an adverse inference even where the defendant explained that he refused to answer police questions as a matter of principle to protest inequities in the administration of justice.[104] Most recently, the House of Lords held that Article 4 of the Order empowers a judge trying a case without a jury to draw adverse inferences from a defendant's refusal to answer questions at trial if the prosecution has made out a *prima facie* case.[105] This case, *Murray v. Director of Public Prosecutions*, stated that for the purpose of drawing a negative inference, a *prima facie* case exists when "aspects of the evidence taken alone or in combination with other facts clearly call for an explanation which the accused ought to be in a position to give."[106]

Defense solicitors greet these developments with understandable concern, for both their clients and themselves. Barra McGrory, for example, pointed out that precisely because negative inferences can now be drawn in certain circumstances, it is all the more important that a detainee have advice of counsel. "What happens now is that the police read a detainee numerous complex rules, and the detainee often cannot understand what his rights are."[107]

B. Access to Lawyers

Rather than protect the right to counsel, emergency provisions specific to solicitors subvert it. The EPA, PTA, and recent case law combine to accomplish this end by restricting access to defense solicitors in obvious and subtle ways. Most directly, the law in Northern Ireland delays access to a solicitor and severely limits it when granted. Other measures prevent individuals from retaining counsel in a free and

---

[104]*R. v. Morrison, Martin, et al.*, Northern Ireland Court of Appeal, (transcript), May 8, 1991.

[105]*Murray v. Director of Public Prosecutions*, House of Lords, (transcript), Oct. 29, 1992.

[106]*Id.*, at 12 (opinion of Lord Slynn of Hadley).

[107]Lawyers Committee interview of Barra McGrory, Sept. 1, 1992.

knowing manner. Judicially-created rules have effectively made challenges to denials of access futile. Finally, petty forms of discrimination against defense solicitors underscore their tenuous position. Officials defend these rules in the name of security. But these justifications, no less than the measures themselves, place lawyers under an unwarranted cloud of suspicion, impede the discharge of their professional duties, and place them at additional risk.

Access Restrictions. Section 45 of the 1991 EPA allows the police to prevent "a person who is detained under the terrorism provisions" from consulting a solicitor for up to 48 hours after the initial arrest, then for successive 48 hour periods afterward until release or charge. [Section 45(1), (5)-(6)] While the detainee awaits legal advice the RUC may begin or continue interrogation with impunity. A delay must be authorized "by an officer of at least the rank of superintendent." [Section 45(5)(a)] To authorize the postponement an officer must have reasonable grounds that a consultation will hamper the police in certain ways [Section 45(8)]; specifically, that it:

(a) will lead to interference with or harm to evidence connected with a scheduled offence or interference with or physical injury to any person; or

(b) will lead to the alerting of any person suspected of having committed such any offence but not yet arrested for it; or

(c) will hinder the recovery of any property obtained as a result of such an offence; or

(d) will lead to the interference with the gathering of information about the commission, preparation or instigation of acts or terrorism; or

(e) by alerting any person, will make it more difficult --

(i) to prevent an act of terrorism; or

(ii) to secure the apprehension, prosecution or conviction of any person in connection with the commission, preparation or instigation of an act of terrorism.

This statute, by singling out lawyers for special security concern, in effect codifies official suspicion of the integrity of defense lawyers. Nor does it end there. Even when access is granted, it amounts to no more than a half hour conference between the solicitor and the detainee, after which a subsequent 48 hour denial of access may be authorized. At no point does the detainee have the right to have the solicitor present during the interrogation. Moreover, an officer of at least the rank of Assistant Chief Constable who has reasonable grounds to suspect the security breaches already set forth, may direct that a solicitor confer with the detainee only "in the sight and hearing of a qualified officer of the uniformed branch of the Royal Ulster Constabulary." [Section 45(10)-(11)] Section 44 places similar restrictions on a detainees' access to a friend or relative.

Solicitors, detainees, and official statistics indicate that the police regularly deny access from 24 to the full 48 hours after arrests under emergency legislation. Each of the lawyers who addressed this point asserted that such delays were a standard feature of their practice. In a sworn affidavit submitted to the High Court of Justice, Barra McGrory went so far as to state that, "It has been my experience that the police have deferred legal access in practically all arrests under section 14 of the Prevention of Terrorism Act 1989 either for 24 hour or 48 hour periods and that immediate access to a Solicitor by a detainee in Castlereagh is now the exception rather than the rule."[108] Statistics bear the last point out. According to the NIO, over half the requests for a solicitor were delayed in 1990 and 1991.[109]

---

[108]*McKenna's Application*, Queen's Bench Division (transcript of judgement by Hutton, LCJ), Feb. 10, 1992, at 36-37.

[109]*See Intimidation of Defence Lawyers in Northern Ireland, supra* note 35, at 9.

Succeeding refusals are also common. Some detainees also complained that they have even been prevented from seeing their solicitor for periods exceeding the statutory period. Patrick McDade, for example, claims that he was not allowed to see his solicitor during his detention just prior to Patrick Finucane's murder even though this lasted for four days. He also claims to have been similarly denied access to a solicitor during a five day detention in 1987.

Joseph Rice, a solicitor who represented one of the UDR Four,[110] pointed out that the difference between the EPA and PACE in this as in other areas is "stark." On this point Rice echoed the remarks of Peter Burns before the (UN) Committee Against Torture.[111] Article 59 of the PACE Order parallels Article 58 of the 1984 PACE Act in effect in England and Wales. Each version of PACE guarantees that a person held in custody may consult a solicitor privately at any time. In practice, this includes the right of the detainee to have a solicitor present throughout interrogation. This critical right applies even to detainees held in England, Scotland, and Wales under the PTA.[112] Further, PACE sets forth grounds for delaying a detainee's access to legal advice that are narrower than those specified by the EPA. Delays are permitted in England and Wales only for "serious arrestable offenses" at the discretion of an officer of at least the rank of superintendent on reasonable grounds that a consultation will interfere with gathering evidence or securing witnesses, will alert other suspects, or will hinder the recovery of property. In no event can the delay exceed 36 hours. Police questioning, moreover, must cease until the consultation has taken place.

R. v. Chambers illustrates what can occur in Northern Ireland because of the gulf between the two regimes. The defendant was first

---

[110]*See* text *infra*, at page 84.

[111]Burns Comments to CAT, *supra* note 99, at 5. *See generally*, "The Police and Criminal Evidence (Northern Ireland) Order 1989 (Symposium)," 40 *Northern Ireland Legal Quarterly* 319 (1989).

[112]Prevention of Terrorism (Temporary Provisions) Act of 1989, Sched. 3, § 7.(1)-(3).

charged for murder under the ordinary criminal law prior to PACE, and then under PACE. Later he was charged for paramilitary activity under the EPA. As a result, the police interrogated him without benefit of a solicitor. The defendant broke down and confessed within the first 48 hours. The charges were then switched back under PACE, but the incriminating statements came in nonetheless, resulting in a conviction. The case is now on appeal.

With regard to international standards, the PTA's restrictions on a detainee's access to legal counsel run directly counter to the UN Basic Principles on the Role of Lawyers. In particular, they are difficult to reconcile with Principle 8, which provides that persons held in custody "*shall* be provided with adequate opportunities, time and facilities to be visited by and to communicate and consult with a lawyers, *without delay*, interception or censorship and in full confidentiality . . . [and that] consultations may be within the sight, but not within the hearing, of law enforcement officials" [emphasis added].

Both UN observers and non-governmental organizations have subjected the PTA's access restrictions to severe criticism. In his 1992 report to the UN Sub-Commission on Prevention of Discrimination and Protection of Minorities, Louis Joinet noted that according to several human rights groups, "exercise of the rights of the defence is appreciably weakened by the emergency legislation . . . which among other things authorizes the police to delay giving detainees access to the services of a lawyer." M. Joinet added that the practice of identifying lawyers with their clients or their clients' causes "makes lawyers vulnerable and seriously weakens the guarantees of protection, and hence the exercise of the rights of defence." Peter Burns, the Country Rapporteur for the (UN) Committee Against Torture has expressed similar sentiments. So, too, has Amnesty International, the Committee on the Administration of Justice, and Helsinki Watch.[113]

---

[113]Louis Joinet, *The Independence and Impartiality of the Judiciary, Jurors and Assessors and the Independence of Lawyers*, UN Sub-Commission on Prevention of Discrimination and Protection of Minorities, 44th Session, UN Doc. E/CN.4/Sub.2/1992/25, at 23 (Aug. 5, 1992); Burns Comments to CAT, *supra* note 99, at 5; Amnesty International, *United Kingdom: Allegations of Ill-Treatment in Northern Ireland*, at 6-7 (Nov. 1991); Committee on the Administration of Justice,

No official with whom we spoke referred to a single instance of a solicitor's contact with a client resulting in any of the consequences set forth in Section 45 of the EPA. Nor would such consequences appear likely given that from 1974 to 1990, only 1.3% of those detained "under the terrorism provisions" were charged with a scheduled offense.[114] These figures bolster one solicitor's observation that the true reason for preventing a detainee from consulting a solicitor is not the fear that he or she will pass information, but a determination to undermine the client's legal rights in order to obtain incriminating information.

<u>Judicial Review Actions</u>. Settled doctrine establishes the availability of judicial review of decisions to delay a detainee access to a solicitor. Recent case law has made this safeguard meaningless. Along the way, it has also put lawyers in an unwarranted ethical position as well as in greater danger.

Lord Templeman summarized the grounds for judicial review in *R. v. IRC, Ex parte Preston*. There he stated, "Judicial review is available where a decision making authority exceeds its powers, commits an error of law, commits a breach of natural justice, reaches a decision which no reasonable tribunal could have reached, or abuses its powers."[115] The same principles apply to denials of access to legal advice.[116] They also apply in Northern Ireland, even under the EPA.[117] Courts in Northern Ireland have held, moreover, that immediate judicial review may provide the only meaningful remedy for

---

Submission to the United Nations Committee Against Torture, at 7-8 (Nov. 13, 1991); Helsinki Watch Report, *supra* note 2, at 30-43.

[114]*Intimidation of Defence Lawyers, supra* note 35, at 9.

[115]*R. v. IRC, Ex parte Preston*, (1985) 1 AC 835, at 862C.

[116]*See, e.g., R. v. Chief Constable of the Avon and Somerset Constabulary, Ex parte Robinson* [1989] 2 All ER 15 (judicial review available for denial of access to solicitor's clerk under Article 58 of the PACE Act).

[117]*See, e.g., McKenna's Application*, High Court of Justice (transcript of judgement by Hutton, LCJ), Feb. 10, 1992.

an improper decision to prevent a detainee from consulting with a solicitor in a timely manner.[118]

An important series of recent cases show that the opportunity for judicial review does not necessarily yield adequate remedies. *McNearney's Application* established the pattern. In this case the High Court of Justice considered a 48 hour denial of immediate access, enjoining interrogation while the case was pending. The court also ruled that the RUC had to come forward with some reasonable justification for the delay. According to Lord Justice Kelly, the RUC satisfied this burden by contending that, in light of the experience of the superintendent in charge, the solicitor could have inadvertently passed a "coded" message between the paramilitary organization and the client.[119] In this regard, *McNearney* followed *R. v. Harper*, where the Northern Ireland Court of Appeal refused to exclude a confession in which restricted access to the solicitor was justified on the same basis.[120]

Defense solicitors successfully fought back in the succeeding case of *Re Duffy's Application*. Here the solicitor denied access lodged an immediate judicial review action, but took the additional step of filing "undertakings" with the RUC and the court that he would not "communicate with any person, in any matter as to what occurred during consultation for the deferred period." The submission to the court continued:

> . . . As an Officer of the Court I have always respected the balance of duties owed clients and the Criminal Justice System. I have never used information received in the course of consultations with a client other than for the legal benefit of my client. I have never used such information in any way that could lead to interference with the gathering of information about the commission,

---

[118]*Id.*

[119]*McNearney's Application*, High Court of Justice, (transcript), Sept. 1991.

[120]*R. v. Harper*, (1990) 4 NIJB 75.

> preparation, or instigation of a crime. . . . It is impossible that any Police Officer could reasonably believe that I could under any circumstances contribute to any of the grounds [specified in the EPA].

The High Court accepted this commitment and granted the solicitor immediate access. The judges reasoned that a solicitor could not unwittingly pass information to paramilitary groups if he or she had undertaken not to pass information to anyone. Lord Chief Justice Hutton, however, left open the possibility that in other cases the police might justifiably decide that an undertaking "could not be relied on," and come forward with specific reasons why.[121]

Two subsequent judgments brought the situation back to square one. They did so by accepting the RUC's position that even where a solicitor had submitted a good faith undertaking, a paramilitary group could still force the solicitor to divulge information through kidnapping and torture. The first case, *In re McKenna and McKenna*, involved a detention of a husband and wife after firearms were found in their house. Upon the denial of access, the McKennas' solicitor, Barra McGrory, immediately lodged a judicial review action accompanied by an undertaking. As the action unfolded, the RUC raised the kidnapping argument. McGrory responded with an affidavit which in part stated that:

> . . . The firm in which I am a partner has acted for over 20 years for many people alleged to have committed serious terrorist crimes. I personally have been in a position to give advice in those matters for a period of seven years and during that time have advised many hundreds of people. . . . It has not been my personal experience nor has it been the experience of any member of this firm that any pressure has been brought to bear by members of terrorist organizations to divulge confidential information.

---

[121]*Re Duffy's Application*, High Court of Justice, (transcript), Sept. 20, 1991.

The Court of Appeal, meeting at 1:30 in the morning, enjoined the interrogation. At a later hearing on the merits, however, the judges accepted the RUC's kidnapping scenario notwithstanding the solicitor's undertaking. In the lead opinion, Lord Chief Justice Hutton reasoned that the police had satisfied their burden of proof "because the Provisional IRA is a completely ruthless and unscrupulous organization which would be fully prepared, by force or threat, against him or his family, to compel Mr McGrory, against his will and in breach of his undertaking, to disclose to it what the applicants had told him in the course of consultation."[122] The Court of Appeal solidified its stance in *In re Kenneway and Others*. Here Lord Chief Justice Hutton and Lord Justice Kelly again accepted that RUC's argument that, notwithstanding the solicitor's undertaking, the IRA might be able to force the lawyer to divulge information. Justice Shiel, who had issued a preliminary injunction against interrogation, dissented.[123]

We find puzzling the willingness of a majority of the judges on the High Court to credit so inherently implausible a threat to the interests set forth in Section 45 of the EPA. It seems more plausible that the judges believe police interrogation should be shielded from interference by defense solicitors. If so, the judges are a part of the problem. They contribute to a general atmosphere in which defense services are denigrated.

Defense solicitors addressed a number of concerns arising out of recent developments in judicial review that go beyond the obvious delay of access to clients. One group of concerns relates to undertakings. *McKenna* and *Kenneway* render the status of the practice unclear. To the extent it does survive, undertakings raise several troubling issues. Perhaps most troubling, undertakings by definition divide a solicitor's duties between the client and the court. As an officer of the court the solicitor must abide by his or her commitment not to disclose information, presumably on pain of contempt. This *ad hoc* duty, however, directly conflicts with the solicitor's obligation to act as a

---

[122] *In re McKenna and McKenna*, QB (transcript of judgement by Hutton, LCJ), at 39, Feb. 10, 1992.

[123] *In re Kenneway and Others*, Northern Ireland Court of Appeal (1992).

zealous advocate, including using information gleaned from an initial consultation to seek exculpatory evidence without delay or simply to relay pressing messages to the detainee's spouse or relatives. Moreover, *Duffy* suggests that the practice still gives the RUC the option of attacking the solicitor's undertaking as insincere. Any such attack of necessity implies that the solicitor may be "unduly sympathetic" to paramilitary organizations. Patrick Finucane's case is a grim reminder of what such an implication may entail.

Further, several solicitors pointed out that the basic structure of the EPA discourages judicial review whatever the judicial gloss. A denial of access under Section 45 by definition means that the police have publicly concluded that permitting a certain named solicitor to see a detainee involves a security risk, implying that the lawyer is in league with the paramilitaries. That implication, moreover, is popularly reinforced every time the press reports that a particular solicitor is challenging a 48 hour delay. It is far less likely that the paramilitaries will engage in kidnapping to obtain release of coded information. Thus, lawyers who pursue judicial review of delays of access will continue to be wrongly identified with their clients by paramilitaries of a different political persuasion.

<u>Limitations on Choice</u>. Another often overlooked problem is choice of counsel. Section 45(1) of the EPA entitles a detainee to consult a solicitor "if he [or she] requests." The RUC apparently interprets this provision to require a detainee to ask for a solicitor or firm specifically. If a detainee fails to do this, he or she can theoretically choose a name from the Legal Aid panelbook, which in effect means any solicitor in town, whether a criminal law practitioner or not. Both the official reason and source for this rule remain obscure.

Less obscure are the obstacles that result. One occurs when an individual being taken into custody asks a spouse or relative to contact a qualified solicitor. Barra McGrory pointed out that when the relation does so, the police frequently bar solicitors from the detention center because the detainee did not request that particular lawyer. Phillip Breen echoed this point. Another difficulty arises because a detainee cannot change his or her choice of solicitor, even on the initiative of the original solicitor. Padraigin Drinan related one instance in which a detainee asked for her because he had heard of her prisoners' rights work. She thought it would have been better for the client to have had P.J. McGrory, on the strength of his long experience, whom Drinan could have secured, to appear in the detention center. Since the detainee had asked for her, however, he lost his chance to speak with the more seasoned lawyer during the crucial period of interrogation.

The RUC's requirement that a detainee under the emergency legislation make a specific request appears to have no counterpart under the PACE Order, but does appear to infringe international guarantees. The UN Basic Principles repeatedly declare that all persons have a right to "a lawyer of their choice." [Numbers 1, 5] The Principles further proclaim that "[g]overnments shall ensure that efficient procedures and responsive mechanism for effective and equal access to lawyers are provided" [Number 2], as well as "ensure that lawyers . . . [are] able to perform all their professional functions without intimidation, hindrance, harassment or improper interference. [Number 16] Far from ensuring a meaningful choice of counsel, the RUC's practice impedes it with no evident justification other than to facilitate interrogation leading to confessions.

Bugging and Other Security Measures. Defense solicitors face additional obstacles, again in the name of security, even when granted access to their clients. Many solicitors take it as a given that conferences with their clients in detention centers are bugged. Peter Madden summed up the common view when, responding to the author of *Big Boys' Rules*, he maintained that, "[n]o lawyer in his right mind would agree to pass a message from a terrorist to his commander because interrogation centers are probably bugged."[124] Solicitors base their suspicions on reports from clients. Madden & Finucane's files show that nearly 10% of the allegations of abuse involve some indication of electronic surveillance of the attorney/client meeting. Often these claims involve interrogators displaying knowledge that could only have been obtained by listening in on consultations. In one typical remark a detainee stated, "[t]he CID man said my story was bullshit and they told me exactly what my solicitor told me. They had obviously bugged the room." Occasionally interrogators are even said to taunt detainees about

---

[124]Letter dated June 8, 1992 from Peter Madden to Mark Urban.

bugging. One detainee, for example, claimed that the police "told me that when I saw my solicitor there would be a supervised visit with an inspector present. . . . They said it didn't matter anyway because it was all taped."

Other intrusions are undisputed. Before entering a court, prison, or a detention center, defense lawyers are routinely subjected to a body search as well as a search of their briefcases. Government attorneys are not searched. The RUC defends this policy as a necessary security measure even though there is no recorded instance of a solicitor smuggling any contraband to any client. Padraigin Drinan did observe that the police had at least ceased the practice of taking photographs of defense solicitors as they went into the Diplock Courts through a different entrance from the government attorneys. As British Irish Rights Watch observed, the current policy at best discriminates against defense solicitors as officers of the court and at worst serves no purpose beyond intimidation.

C. Detention Practices and Conditions

Further evidence indicates that the actual conditions within the detention centers make a bad situation worse. Such centers occupy the front lines in the official battle to garner information, informers, and confessions. As such, they are designed to be coercive. Thus, they are also almost completely devoid of the most basic mechanisms for insuring that abuse against detainees -- or their solicitors -- does not take place. Once more the authorities defend existing procedures citing security concerns. These concerns amount to little more than generalized speculations. There are, however, specific, repeated, and credible allegations of mistreatment.

Overview. One solicitor described the setting in which interrogations are conducted as "oppressive, indeed Victorian." The former detainees who spoke to our mission presented accounts that were not only consistent with one another but with the findings of previous human rights missions.[125] Patrick McDade, detained 13 times, described a typical experience:

> I was arrested at 5:30 a.m. I was then brought to a cell with no windows, where it was impossible to tell day from night. The lighting consisted of one bulb that was on at all times. The cell was about 6' by 8' and had a leather bed. After I was brought to the cell, I was sent to see a doctor for an exam, then brought back.
>
> The interrogation began at around 9:30 and went to about 12:30. (I could tell the time by looking at the interrogators watches.) The interrogation room was about 7' by 7' and consisted of a table, three chairs, and a heater. The standard was for two detectives to conduct the interview. After [two hours of interrogation involving mistreatment], there was a break [for lunch]. The questioning began again with two different detectives and went from 1:30 to 5:30. This session was more of the same. Then came dinner, which was followed by another session from 7:30 to 11:30. Again there were two different detectives and again the questioning was more of the same.[126]

This detention, McDade's first, lasted for three days.

Accounts from detainees are also replete with stories of physical and psychological abuse. McDade alleged that he was slapped, prodded with a boot, knocked off his chair, threatened and insulted throughout his detention. Paul Finnegan maintained that his interrogators beat him,

---

[125] *See, e.g.*, Lawyers Committee interviews of Seamus Finucane, Brian Austin, Paul Finnegan, Aug. 31, 1992; and interviews of Geraldine O'Connor and John Pierce, Sept. 3, 1992. For reports on alleged abuses in detention centers, *see infra*, note 128.

[126] Lawyers Committee interview of Patrick McDade, Aug. 31, 1992.

slapped him, kicked him in the testicles, and lifted him by his head.[127] Alleged mistreatment of detainees is beyond the scope of this particular Lawyers Committee mission.[128] It is nonetheless apparent that these credible claims not only serve to corroborate charges that solicitors suffer abuse, but also suggest that the safeguards against abuse of detainees are grossly inadequate.

Monitoring Interrogation. A prime example of the lack of sufficient protection for detainees is the RUC's system of closed circuit television monitors. Currently each detention center has cameras installed in the interrogation rooms but not in either the cells or corridors. Uniformed officers who are not part of the interrogation team are supposed to observe the questioning on screens placed in another room and report on any mistreatment. One officer must attempt to watch several monitors at a time. None of the proceedings are recorded in any way. The RUC justifies this policy by asserting that either audio- or videotaping could make it easier for a paramilitary group to find out whether a detainee provided the police with off-the-record information. That would be true, of course, only if a tape were produced in open court in response to a charge of improper interrogation. Only the detainee could make such a charge, and the detainee would hardly be likely to do so knowing that his or her informer status would thereby be disclosed. Like "the fear of kidnapping" justification for denying access to solicitors, we view the police's reasons for not videotaping interrogations as pretextual.

The results of the Northern Ireland interrogation system are not unexpected. Detainees report that detectives freely taunt them about the cameras, saying that they are not working, that the detectives can turn

---

[127]Lawyers Committee interview of Paul Finnegan, Aug. 31, 1992.

[128]Observers and groups that have focussed on this problem, however, have found allegations of mistreatment to be numerous and serious. *See, e.g.*, Burns Comments to CAT, *supra* note 99, at 7-8; Amnesty International, *Allegations of Ill-Treatment in Northern Ireland*, *passim* (Nov. 1991); Amnesty International, *United Kingdom: Human Rights Concerns*, at 2-11 (June 1991); Committee on the Administration of Justice, *Submission to the United Nations Committee Against Torture*, at 3-6 (Nov. 13, 1991); Committee on the Administration of Justice, *Human Rights in Northern Ireland*, at 15-16 (Feb. 1991); Helsinki Watch Report, *supra* note 2, at 11-43.

them off or on, or that the officer watching them couldn't care less about what happens to the suspect. In one instance, Geraldine O'Connor reported that a detective hung his jacket over the camera during an entire session, telling her that no one used the cameras anyway. To date, the closed circuit surveillance system has not yielded a single disciplinary proceeding concerning mistreatment during interrogation.

Few outside the RUC consider the surveillance system effective. In speaking with our delegation, Lord Colville reaffirmed his earlier call for at least silent videotaping. He maintained that the RUC's security concerns, which he chose to credit despite their implausibility, could be addressed by placing the camera in the center of the ceiling to prevent lipreading. Charles Hill QC, told us that one of the main goals of his tenure as the chairman of Standing Advisory Commission for Human Rights (SACHR) was to get a system of silent videotaping instituted (presumably with cameras as currently placed, at an angle from the side). Mr. Hill pointed out that an additional difficulty of taping would be a defendant's ability to have a silent video played in court, though it was not clear why the rules of evidence could not be amended to address this concern.[129] As for audio-recording of interrogations, trial schemes are underway in both Northern Ireland and England under PACE. Lord Colville said that he was awaiting the results of these experiments before taking a position on sound recording, though he did point out that audiotaping made retribution easier.

The fears surrounding either type of recording appear to us specious. Officials failed to cite any concrete instance of retribution arising out of the current experiments or on the basis of the interrogation notes currently kept. Perhaps that is because those notes are deliberately made incomplete. The recent UDR Four case suggests as much.

Note Taking. The RUC has recently adopted one modest reform. During the Lawyers Committee's visit, the police announced the implementation of a system for electronic timing of note taking.

---

[129]Lawyers Committee interview of Charles Hill QC and Dennis Carson, Sept. 3, 1992. *See* Standing Advisory Commission for Human Rights, *Report for 1991-1992*, at 219-220; Charles Hill QC, "Video Recording of Interviews During Police Detention" (1991).

Electronic timing helps prevent subsequent alteration of notes by providing a record of when they were taken.

This reform almost certainly grew out of the UDR Four scandal. This case involved the conviction of four Protestant members of the Ulster Defense Regiment for the sectarian murder of Adrian Carroll. The Court of Appeal overturned three of these convictions when Electro Static Detection Apparatus (ESDA) analysis, a forensic device for detecting whether records were altered, proved that police interrogation notes had been falsified to incriminate the suspects.[130] Significantly, ESDA analysis further revealed that the RUC deleted a request made by one of the soldiers, James Hegan, to see a solicitor.[131] The reversals in the UDR Four case in part resulted from a campaign for justice led by Ian Paisley, Jr., the son of the unionist MP and a civil rights advocate. In a meeting with members of our delegation, Mr. Paisley stressed that the UDR Four case showed that concern about interrogation abuses cuts across sectarian lines. He welcomed any reforms the RUC instituted, but added that the most effective safeguards would be audiotaping, videotaping, and immediate access to solicitors as under PACE.[132]

Lay Visitors. Currently, no one other than a member of the RUC monitors the closed circuit television screens in the detention centers. For detentions under the PACE Order in Northern Ireland, a lay visitors plan has recently been introduced which parallels a system long established in England and Wales under the PACE Act. Under this plan, appointed members of the public visit police stations on a regular but unannounced basis. Lord Colville stated that such a system was worth attempting with detainees under the emergency legislation. He further suggested that either magistrates or solicitors would make sensible lay visitors.

---

[130] *R. v. Latimer, Hegan, Bell, and Allen*, Northern Ireland Court of Appeal, (transcript), 1991.

[131] *Id.*, at 109-10, 112-14.

[132] Lawyers Committee interview of Ian Paisley, Jr., Sept. 1, 1992.

The NIO informed our delegation that a variant of the lay visitors plan would be established in the near future.[133] This occurred in December 1992, when the government announced the appointment of Sir Louis Blom-Cooper QC to the newly created post of Independent Commissioner for Holding Centers. The Independent Commissioner will have authority to make unannounced visits to holding centers in order to provide an independent check that persons detained in interrogation centers on suspicion of paramilitary activity are treated fairly.[134] It is not clear why the government feels that the current appointees as potential lay visitors under the PACE Order are not satisfactory. The Lawyers Committee nonetheless welcomes this development as a positive step and expresses its hope that the Independent Commissioner will prove effective.

D. Complaints Procedures and Other Remedies

The ultimate test for any legal regime is its accountability for abuses that do arise. Few solicitors in Northern Ireland consider the system accountable. This skepticism results from what the police refer to as their "constitutional" position. The RUC answers to neither the "government," in the sense of officials answerable to elected representatives, nor to a "bill of rights," in the sense of guarantees enforceable by judicial review that cannot be changed by ordinary legislation.[135] Instead, the police are responsible to "the law and the courts."

The "law," however, is an abstraction. In Northern Ireland it is also an abstraction that often foments human rights abuses in the first place. As for the courts, the bench possesses few institutional

---

[133]Lawyers Committee interview of John Ledlie, Nicholas Perry, David Lavery, David McIroy at the Northern Ireland Office, Sept. 3, 1992.

[134]Letter dated Jan. 23, 1993 from Sir Louis Blom-Cooper QC to Michael Posner, Lawyers Committee for Human Rights.

[135]Conversely, the United Kingdom is subject to international human rights instruments like the European Convention on Human Rights. These instruments, however, are not enforceable in U.K. courts unless Parliament incorporates them into domestic law.

mechanisms to hold the police accountable other than dicta,[136] civil damage actions, and Coroner's Inquests. The Director of Public Prosecutions (DPP), as an officer of the courts charged with upholding the law, may bring criminal prosecutions. But the prosecutor, though independent of the police and accountable to the Attorney General in London, has no means of investigating misconduct by the security forces except through the RUC. Not surprisingly, the complaints procedures established under this framework are ineffective. In this setting the RUC is not so much accountable to the law as a law unto itself.

RUC. In general, only the RUC can investigate complaints against the RUC. An allegation may be initially lodged with either the police or the ICPC, though in either case they will be forwarded to the Chief Constable. When the complaint relates to a junior officer, and is not suitable for informal resolution, the Chief Constable must appoint an officer to conduct a formal investigation and notify the ICPC. The Investigating Officer will usually be from the RUC's Complaints and Discipline Branch, will normally be two ranks above the officer investigated, and cannot come from that officer's same branch or sub-division.[137] Completed investigation reports are sent to the Chief Constable, who then decides whether to forward the matter to the DPP for criminal prosecution, to bring internal disciplinary proceedings, or to do nothing. Disciplinary charges, like criminal accusations, must be proven beyond a reasonable doubt.

The procedures vary in special situations. When a complaint relates to an officer above the rank of Chief Superintendent, responsibility for the matter falls to the Police Authority, a body of 16 to 22 individuals appointed by the Secretary of State which is responsible for maintaining an adequate and efficient police force for Northern Ireland. Investigations may also arise out of media allegations or from

---

[136]*See, e.g., R. v. Latimer, Hegan, Bell, and Allen* (transcript of judgement), 1991.

[137]The RUC's rankings are as follows: Chief Constable; Deputy Chief Constable; Assistant Chief Constable; Chief Superintendent; Superintendent; Chief Inspector; Inspector; Sergeant; Constable. Officers with either of the last two ranks usually conduct interrogation in the detention centers.

politicians even when there is no complainant. In extraordinary situations, the Chief Constable may request a high-ranking officer from another U.K. police force to conduct a special investigation such as the Stalker/Sampson "Shoot-to-Kill" and Stevens "Collusion" Inquiries. Even in these inquiries, only RUC officers could actually make arrests.[138]

These procedures do little to overcome the obvious problems that go with self-policing. They are especially inadequate given the historic position of the RUC. The 90% Protestant make-up of the force makes it one of the last places many members of the Catholic and nationalist communities would turn to seek help for any problems, much less complaints against its officers. The constant paramilitary attacks against the force make it unlikely that many officers would vigorously pursue allegations perceived by them to come from the same quarters as the attacks. It is hardly surprising that in these circumstances solicitors who represent clients the police seek to put away make little use of the current system.

ICPC. This is so despite the creation of the ICPC. The ICPC was established in 1988 by the Police (Northern Ireland) Order 1987 to provide independent oversight over complaints investigations. The Commission is made of up eight members appointed by the Secretary of State; four are solicitors and one other has legal training. According to James Grew, the Commission's chairman, the ICPC is balanced between male and female, Protestant and Catholic.[139]

The Commission may supervise investigations, but cannot initiate or conduct investigations itself. The only way it can become involved other than as a result of individual complaints is at the request of the Secretary of State, the Police Authority, or the Chief Constable. The ICPC must supervise in cases resulting in serious physical injury or death. It can elect to supervise in all other cases.

---

[138] *See* CAJ, *Civil Liberties, supra* note 90, at 55-66.

[139] Lawyers Committee interview of James Grew, Chairman, ICPC, and Brian G. McClelland, Secretary, ICPC, Sept. 3, 1992.

Supervision has several components. As an initial matter, the ICPC can accept or reject the RUC's choice of investigating officers. A Commission member is then appointed to the case, and this overseer meets with the investigating officer to go over a plan of action. The supervising Commission member may also dictate how certain aspects of the investigation proceed, such as requiring additional staff or directing that certain people be interviewed. The supervisor cannot, however, become directly involved other than attending interviews as a silent observer.

Once the investigation is complete, the Commission as a whole has the power to issue or withhold a "statement of satisfaction." The ICPC can also forward the report to the DPP, who decides whether to bring criminal charges, or direct that disciplinary charges be brought if the Chief Constable has failed to do so.[140]

Charles Hill of SACHR told our delegation that lawyers should not give up on the ICPC. He nonetheless admitted that the system had evident weakness. Perhaps most important, the Commission lacks remedial power apart from refusing to accept an investigation report. At most, repeated refusal might embarrass the RUC politically and even prompt a Parliamentary Question to the Secretary of State. Neither check, however, has proven effective or even been attempted. Other deficiencies include the Commission's inability to commence investigations or to play a more direct role in inquiries that are underway. Even with these powers the ICPC would also confront the high standard of proof -- beyond a reasonable doubt -- for disciplinary charges. In part for these reasons, in the past four years not one police officer has been disciplined as a result of a complaint arising out of detention under emergency legislation. Absent substantial reforms, the question remains why solicitors should continue to try using the system.

<u>Coroner's Inquests</u>. The Coroner offers one of the only independent checks on police conduct that also has independent investigatory authority. Coroners and Deputy Coroners are judicial

---

[140]*See* CAJ, *Civil Liberties, supra* note 90, at 60-61; Lawyers Committee interview with James Grew, Chairman, ICPC, and Brian G. McClelland, Secretary, ICPC, Sept. 3, 1992.

officers appointed by the Lord Chancellor under the Coroner's Act (Northern Ireland) of 1959. The Coroner's chief duties include: investigating sudden or unexplained deaths; establishing their medical cause; and determining the surrounding facts and circumstances. To do this, the Coroner conducts inquests, often with a jury, where he or she can issue a summons for witnesses and compel testimony. Relatives of the deceased, along with other "properly interested persons," may also question witnesses. As is true in Britain, Northern Ireland Coroners do not attempt to allocate responsibility, although the evidence the Coroner uncovers may point to the responsible party.[141]

The Coroner's inquest has a potential role in protecting lawyers in several regards. Should a lawyer ever again be murdered, the inquest would provide the only public forum for discovering evidence, such as the murder weapon, that could establish official involvement in the death. To date, most of the available evidence concerning the Finucane killing comes from the Coroner's inquiry. In addition, an inquest may turn up evidence suggesting collusion by the security forces in the murder of a solicitor's client. If the client and the solicitor had both been the subjects of previous death threats -- something that the inquest would not establish -- the solicitor could take additional precautions and other appropriate action.

In the words of one solicitor, the current Coroner's inquest process is nonetheless "prehistoric." One deficiency involves the lack of Legal Aid for the families of victims. A number of lawyers observed that the Legal Aid system should be extended to cover Coroner's inquests. Joseph Rice, for example, recalled that at the Craigavon "shoot-to-kill" inquest, three solicitors representing the families of the deceased *pro bono* faced about 30 government lawyers. He added that even he and his colleagues could only help so much since, as a practical matter, it is impossible for them to bring in pathologists and other forensic experts on a *pro bono* basis. A related problem involves discovery. Currently neither surviving family members nor their solicitors have the power to conduct discovery in order to determine

[141]Northern Ireland Court Service, *The Work of the Coroner in Northern Ireland: Some Questions Answered* (1991).

what evidence may be available and relevant to pursue in the inquest itself.[142]

Two further concerns relate to the Coroner's exercise of discretion in admitting evidence and the scope of his or her mandate to do so. A Coroner may exercise his or her discretion to exclude evidence that is not relevant to the purposes of the inquest. If those purposes are interpreted narrowly, significant evidence may never appear on the public record. On this point the Finucane inquest is suggestive. There the Coroner ruled that evidence relating to previous death threats would be excluded as irrelevant.

As an initial matter, the Coroner should interpret the traditionally understood purposes for conducting inquests more broadly. In addition, Parliament should clarify and expand the statutory purposes of the Coroner's inquest to render narrow rulings more difficult in the future. The Coroner's Act assumes but does not spell out what aspects of an unexplained death an inquest should examine. The Act does, however, suggest one formula for determining what evidence is relevant in specifying one of the grounds for the mandatory summoning of a jury. This ground arises when "the death occurred in circumstances the continuance or possible recurrence of which is prejudicial to the health or safety of the public or any section of the public."[143] Established as a ground to admit evidence, this definition -- or a modified version -- would provide a basis to explore evidence of official threats insofar as they prejudiced public safety in general, and the safety of detainees and solicitors in particular.

Finally, it is especially ironic that a further flaw in the system was resurrected by the reversal of one of Patrick Finucane's major accomplishments. As noted, Finucane brought an appeal from a Coroner's ruling that members of the security forces involved in a killing could merely submit affidavits rather than testify under oath subject to questioning. As a result, the Court of Appeal held that the police could be called to testify. The House of Lords, however, reversed the Court

---

[142]Lawyers Committee interview of Joseph Rice, Sept. 3, 1992.

[143]Coroners Act (Northern Ireland) 1959, § 18(1)(e).

of Appeal and let stand the original rule. In this way an effective device for holding the police accountable was eliminated.[144]

Law Society. The Law Society is not a governmental institution, but it does have a responsibility for insuring governmental accountability. The UN Basic Principles on the Role of Lawyers direct that, "[p]rofessional associations of lawyers shall co-operate with Governments to ensure that everyone has effective and equal access to legal services and that lawyers are able, without improper interference, to counsel and assist their clients in accordance with the law and recognized professional standards and ethics." [Number 25]

As an organization, the Law Society has not effectively discharged these duties. This is not to say that certain solicitors have not used the association to pursue legal defense concerns. Presidents of the Law Society for years have raised concerns with the authorities through private meetings and correspondence. By the admission even of those who have pursued it, little has come of this approach. What is currently lacking is any formalized procedures or committees that can assess complaints from solicitors and then pursue the matter with the authorities publicly with the weight of the organization behind solicitors who file credible complaints. Establishing such mechanisms in the past has proven difficult given the apathy of the vast majority of solicitors who do not engage in criminal practice. For the sake of colleagues who face the dangers, abuses, and emergency provisions that this report has described, that apathy must give way to the professional obligation that the UN Principles embody.

---

[144]*See supra* discussion at page 44. For a general critique of Coroner's inquest process, *see* Committee on the Administration of Justice, *Human Rights in Northern Ireland*, at 9-10 (Feb. 1991).

APPENDICES

Appendix A:	Comments of January 1993 by the Northern Ireland Office on the Draft Report "Human Rights and Legal Defence in Northern Ireland" to the Lawyers Committee
Appendix B:	Letter dated January 25, 1993 from Deputy Chief Constable Michael McAtamney, Royal Ulster Constabulary, to Michael Posner, Lawyers Committee for Human Rights

LAWYERS COMMITTEE FOR HUMAN RIGHTS

DRAFT REPORT ON
HUMAN RIGHTS AND LEGAL DEFENCE IN NORTHERN IRELAND

COMMENTS BY THE NORTHERN IRELAND OFFICE

1. The Northern Ireland Office welcomes the opportunity to engage in dialogue with groups such as the Lawyers Committee; even where we have to agree to differ, we believe the process to be a valuable one for both sides. We were impressed by the amount of ground the Committee was able to cover on your necessarily brief visit here, and the speed with which you have assembled your report. Inevitably, given the constraints within which you have had to operate, the report concentrates heavily on the particular issue under investigation; had time allowed, it might have been helpful to include information which would have helped to set the whole question in a broader context. In particular, we feel that the draft report underestimates the seriousness of the terrorist threat here, and the all too real difficulties facing the security forces and the judicial system in coping with a sustained campaign of political and sectarian violence.

2. The report also struck us as, in places, lacking in balance and excessively dependent on uncorroborated allegations and anecdotal material. We accept that in many cases you are simply repeating the allegations of others: and that the Lawyers Committee approaches the issues from a particular, and strongly held, viewpoint. But that perfectly valid perspective seems to us on occasion to spill over into partisanship, reflected in the use of loaded language and the inclusion of value judgements at various points in the text. We particularly believe that the report, especially in the section on Mr Finucane's murder, is unfair to the security forces, and especially to the Royal Ulster Constabulary. Like any organisation, the police are not above criticism: but the force deserves better than the treatment it receives in parts of your paper. Unsubstantiated allegations are no substitute for evidence, particularly in view of the very serious charges you lay at the RUC's door. The report relies heavily on the views of a comparatively small number of people, both within the legal profession and outside it: it is not clear that you have sought sufficiently to balance this testimony with the very different views held by many others here working in the security area.

4. The report's judgements and tone are of course a matter for you, and it is not for the Northern Ireland Office to attempt to

ID 42507

re-draft it. We have, however, set out in general terms below the Government's view on some of the issues you raise, as well as picking up one or two particular points which are factually wrong. (Independent bodies such as the Law Society and Bar Council will, we presume also be commenting to you direct.) The comments are organised by sections, as is the report itself. We have also taken the liberty, since it relates to his responsibilities, of showing the draft report to Sir Louis Blom-Cooper, recently appointed by the Secretary of State as Independent Commissioner for the Holding Centres: I enclose a letter from him to you.

Introduction

5. We have no particular difficulties with your outline of the historical background to Northern Ireland's problems, which seems to us to be broadly correct - albeit written from a viewpoint which not everyone here would accept. We would, however, make the following particular comments:

a. You refer to the position of defence lawyers as being "fraught with peril" and "hazardous". This may be so: but statistically it is less hazardous than being, for example, a member of the judiciary, a member of the security forces or a member of other occupations in Northern Ireland. Further, the situation of defence lawyers is by no means as uniquely dangerous as you imply, even within the legal profession: judges, magistrates and prosecution lawyers (and members of their families) have also been murdered.

b. In the first paragraph on page 4, you should point out that, while the Chief Constable is in the lead on operational matters, security policy is the responsibility of the Secretary of State for Northern Ireland. The Army's subordination to the police is genuine rather than 'nominal'; and the GOC is responsible, through the Chief of the General Staff in London, to an elected politician, the Secretary of State for Defence. (The GOC is also, of course, the Northern Ireland Secretary's senior military adviser.)

c. In footnote 11, you should perhaps point out that currently only one of the UK's derogations from the ECHR is maintained.

d. You might make some reference in the section on emergency legislation to the elaborate safeguards which also exist, including the need for Parliament to renew the PTA and EPA annually, and the annual review of the legislation by an independent reviewer.

Section 1: Intimidation

6. The attitude of both the Government and the RUC to the sort of behaviour you allege in this section is unequivocal. If such behaviour takes place, it is totally unacceptable. In order to take effective action against any officers who may be behaving improperly, however, it is first necessary to produce evidence to support the accusations. If those you have interviewed have such evidence, then we hope you will encourage them to come forward. The repetition of unsubstantiated allegations is neither helpful nor fair to the police officers concerned.

7. Turning to particular points within this section, we would make the following comments:

a. In the first paragraph on page 10, you report the view of "detainees, solicitors and journalists" that the security forces in Northern Ireland "violate basic international standards safeguarding the role of lawyers". In the next sentence you describe Mr Finucane's murder as "simply the most heinous instance of systematic harassment of defence lawyers". The impression given is that the security forces murdered Mr Finucane (despite the fact that in the previous paragraph you in fact quote the UFF's statement that they carried out the killing): which is how many people will read the paragraph. Similarly, later in this section you refer to the murders of McGuire and O'Prey, quoting unsubstantiated allegations that they had been threatened by the police and then recording the fact that both had been killed by loyalists, the implication being that they were, at the least, 'set up' by the police. Where is the evidence to support either of these implied but extremely serious allegations? There are a number of occasions throughout the report where different events are linked in the text to give the misleading impression that they are connected in reality, without any evidence of such a connection being deployed.

b. On page 17, you refer to Lord Colville as an

'official'. He is not: he is currently the independent reviewer of the PTA and EPA. As such his work is independent of Government.

c. Your statement on page 20 that the religious composition of the RUC "complicates matters", in that the force is largely Protestant, surprised us, as we had understood the report to be suggesting that defence lawyers were intimidated regardless of their religious and political background.

Section II: The Murder of Patrick Finucane

8. In this section you make extremely grave allegations of security force collusion with loyalist terrorists in Mr Finucane's murder, and claim at the top of page 23 to have 'credible evidence' to this effect. The RUC's investigations into the murder are continuing: it would therefore be inappropriate for us to comment in detail on the case itself. Nevertheless, we would agree that, in order to justify your claims, credible evidence needs to be forthcoming. In the draft report no evidence at all seems to be presented to support your allegations, though you do relate some of the 'staggering array of stories, incidents, and theories' relating to the case. The origins of these stories appear to be Brian Nelson's 'diary', which may or may not be genuine; a series of unnamed 'independent' or 'reliable' sources; and a Channel 4 documentary which, as you note, has been sceptically received by a number of experienced journalists. As we see it, this scarcely justifies your conclusion that there is 'sufficient evidence of the security forces' prior knowledge of the murder plot and encouragement of it', to justify an independent public inquiry: and in this regard we would point particularly to the Stevens Inquiry's finding, which you also record, that 'no evidence was found substantiating the allegation, but rather substantial evidence to the contrary'. The fact that no one has yet been charged with Mr Finucane's murder does not bear the interpretation that you appear to give it - that the RUC are not pursuing the investigation in a professional manner. We presume that you are not suggesting that charges be brought on the basis of insufficient evidence. As we pointed out to you during your visit, there are, tragically, many as yet unsolved murders in Northern Ireland. If you, or those you have spoken to, have evidence that could help solve this particular crime, we would urge that it be passed on to the police as a matter of urgency.

Section III: Lawyers and the Legal Framework

9. In this section you comment on various aspects of the emergency legislation. It is a regrettable fact that the situation in Northern Ireland means that the powers available under this legislation remain fundamental to our efforts to defeat terrorism. We always attempt to strike a proper balance between the security forces' requirement for powers that will enable them to deal effectively with terrorism, and the need to provide effective safeguards for those who may become subject to these emergency provisions. We do not accept the suggestion that the emergency legislation "all but ordains" the intimidation of defence lawyers, or that the law "encourages" hostility to defence lawyers.

As far as the particular comments are concerned:

a. **Extensions of detention**. The Government's position is that the particular difficulties relating to the investigation of terrorism make the exceptional period of a maximum 7 days' detention essential. It is comparatively rare for suspects to be held for the full period; but in certain circumstances, where the most serious terrorist crimes are involved, the police require extensions to be granted in order to complete their enquiries, to have forensic tests carried out, and to validate the information which they have received about a crime.

b. **Confessions**. Any ill-treatment of persons in custody is wholly unacceptable. Stringent safeguards are in place to prevent this, and any police officer acting improperly may face criminal charges and/or disciplinary proceedings. I was glad to note your acknowledgement of the Courts' wide discretion under the EPA to exclude confessions where the prosecution is unable to satisfy them that these were not obtained as a result of torture, inhuman or degrading treatment, or the use or threat of violence: or to avoid unfairness or in the interests of justice. You might care to make the additional point that police reliance on confession evidence is a direct result of the systematic intimidation (and murder) of prosecution witnesses, and the terrorists' increasing skill in eliminating forensic evidence.

c. **Right to silence**. The Criminal Evidence (NI) Order 1988 does not "effectively eliminate the right to silence". It does not affect the presumption of innocence, nor does it shift or lower the burden of proof. The Order does not permit the accused to be convicted on the basis of inferences from silence alone, and the courts are not obliged to draw inferences from silence in all cases: indeed in a number of important cases they have refrained from doing so. The Order does not oblige anyone to speak, and silence is not an offence under it. It does, however, seek to thwart the orchestrated refusal of members of terrorist organisations to answer any substantive questions while in police custody.

d. **Access to lawyers**. The Government recognises that the statutory rights of access to legal advice for those detained in police custody should not be delayed unnecessarily, but believes that in certain circumstances delay is necessary to prevent possible interference with police investigations into of fences, especially terrorist of fences. The EPA, as you know, sets out detailed safeguards and specific grounds which must be present before any delay can be authorised. You are aware of the care with which the Courts have considered the issue.

e. **Monitoring interviews**. We accept that the arguments for and against video-taping are finely balanced. The Government has considered this issue very carefully, however, and shares the view of the police that the recording of interviews would not be appropriate at this juncture. It seems clear that in the circumstances which exist in Northern Ireland suspects would be less prepared to offer vital information to the police if they believed that a permanent record was being made of their co-operation. These fears are real enough: nine people were murdered in 1992 by loyalist and republican terrorists as alleged informers.

f. **Note-taking**. We are glad that you welcome the recent changes announced by the RUC in regard to time-locking and storing interview notes.

g. **Complaints**. Proper mechanisms exist for the investigation of complaints against the security forces. The Independent Commission for Police Complaints must supervise the investigation of complaints involving death or serious injury, and has the discretion to supervise those investigations not requiring its mandatory supervision. The true test of complaints investigations is whether or not there is sufficient evidence to sustain them: if those to whom you have spoken have evidence of police or Army misconduct, then we would hope that they will provide this to the appropriate authorities. Police officers are of course entitled to the same rights as any other citizen: proof of criminal or disciplinary offences must be beyond all reasonable doubt.

Section IV: Recommendations

10. It would be inappropriate for us to comment on the reports' specific recommendations.

Conclusion

11. You and your colleagues have addressed a subject which has caused some concern here: and parts of your report raise important questions. Clearly the rights of defence lawyers and their clients must be protected: this is central to a system of justice. But it seems to us that the overall tone of the report is not completely impartial nor totally balanced. Its value is perhaps somewhat undermined by an apparent reliance on uncorroborated allegations. In particular, we believe that the nature of the section on the murder of Mr Finucane obscures some of the issues raised in the sections preceding and following it.

12. We recognise that some of the above comments are severe. We hope, however, that the Lawyers' Committee will take them in the spirit in which they are meant - namely that of constructive criticism. If the Committee have any further questions, we would be glad to try and deal with them.

NORTHERN IRELAND OFFICE January 1993

Telephone
BELFAST 650222

M. McAtamney C.B.E., Q.P.M., LL.B.
Deputy Chief Constable

BROOKLYN
KNOCK ROAD
BELFAST
NORTHERN IRELAND BT5 6LE

25 January 1993

FEB 0 2 1993

Dear Mr. Fisher.

Thank you for the courtesy of furnishing me with a copy of your draft report. Regrettably, I must convey to you my deep sense of dismay and disappointment that, as it stands, the report falls far short of the balance, fairness, depth and context which the sensitive and complex situation in Northern Ireland requires. Rather than illuminating the situation, I fear the report will exacerbate the difficulties and contribute further to divisiveness and unjustifiable contention.

The shortcomings of the draft report are such as to lead me to the conclusion that it does not merit detailed comment and in its present form is not capable of being constructively amended. Among its many defects, there is a repetition of unsubstantiated allegations, as if these constituted evidence of Security Forces or official misconduct. One is left with the distinct impression of a mass of allegations resting on a limited, unrepresentative base of sources. It is a pity that notwithstanding the assistance made available to the compilers of the report, the end result should be so flawed.

A particularly serious disservice is done to the agencies responsible for the administration of justice and law enforcement in Northern Ireland in that there is no acknowledgement of their sacrifices or the continuing risks they face in striving to uphold democratic values and restore peace. In addition to the late Mr Finucane, with whom your report is particularly concerned, six members of the legal profession (judges, magistrates, a prosecutor) have been murdered, as has also the daughter of a magistrate. Nor is mention made of the fact that 287 police officers have been murdered and a further 7,000 injured.

Illustrative also of the report's defects is your misinterpretation of the law governing the admissibility of confessions. In the recent case of R v Nash, where confession evidence was rejected and the defendant found not guilty, the Lord Chief Justice reviewed the legal position as follows:

"However, in order for his confessions in this case to be excluded from evidence, Nash does not have to satisfy me at the end of the day on the balance of probabilities that he was assaulted by one or more of the interviewing officers. Nash having given prima facie evidence of assault, the onus now rests on the prosecution to satisfy me beyond a reasonable doubt that Nash was not subjected to assault in the course of an interview to induce him to make a confession and I hold that the prosecution has failed to discharge that onus. Accordingly I exclude his confessions from evidence."

"I am satisfied that that part of Nash's case is completely false and on that aspect of the case he told a constant series of lies. However, under our law, even if confessions are true, it is the duty of the judge to exclude them from evidence unless, the issue having been raised, he is satisfied that they were not obtained by violence or other forms of objectionable behaviour specified in Section 11 of the 1991 Act."

"Therefore, even though I do not believe the evidence of Nash that he invented his confessions to the police, the law requires me to exclude those confessions from evidence because I am not satisfied beyond a reasonable doubt that they were not induced by violence." (Lord Chief Justice, Northern Ireland).

You should also be informed that the majority of accused persons appearing before Diplock Courts charged with terrorist-type offences, plead guilty. In 1990, 82 per cent pleaded guilty and of those who contested the charges, 36 per cent were found not guilty; in 1991, 81 per cent pleaded guilty and in contested cases 44 per cent were found not guilty.

I regret that it should be necessary for me to write in these terms; unfortunately the tenor and content of your report leaves me with no alternative. Whilst the RUC is not above criticism, we do have a right to expect fairness and in that respect the report signally fails.

Yours sincerely

Michael McAtamney

Deputy Chief Constable

M Posner Esq
Executive Director
Lawyers Committee for Human Rights
330 Seventh Avenue
10th Floor
New York
New York 10001